LIFE OR DEATH

OTHER TITLES IN THE
UNDERSTANDING CANADIAN LAW SERIES

CRIME SCENE INVESTIGATIONS
FREEDOM OF EXPRESSION
YOUTH AND THE LAW

LIFE OR DEATH:
A MATTER OF CHOICE?

UNDERSTANDING CANADIAN LAW

DANIEL J. BAUM

DUNDURN
TORONTO

Editor: Michael Melgaard
Design: BJ Weckerle
Cover design: Carmen Giraudy
Printer: Webcom

Library and Archives Canada Cataloguing in Publication

Baum, Daniel Jay, 1934-, author
    Life or death : a matter of choice? / Daniel J. Baum.

(Understanding Canadian law series ; 4)
Includes bibliographical references and index. Issued in print and electronic formats.
ISBN 978-1-4597-2378-8 (paperback).--ISBN 978-1-4597-3058-8 (pdf).--
ISBN 978-1-4597-3059-5 (epub)

    1. Patients--Legal status, laws, etc.--Canada. 2. Medical care--Law and legislation--Canada. 3. Euthanasia--Law and legislation--Canada. 4. Right to die--Law and legislation--Canada. I. Title. II. Series: Understanding Canadian law (Toronto, Ont.) ; 4

KE3648.B38 2015   344.7104'19   C2015-903951-7
KF3823.B38 2015   C2015-903952-5

1 2 3 4 5   19 18 17 16 15

 Conseil des Arts du Canada   Canada Council for the Arts   ONTARIO ARTS COUNCIL / CONSEIL DES ARTS DE L'ONTARIO / an Ontario government agency / un organisme du gouvernement de l'Ontario

We acknowledge the support of the **Canada Council for the Arts** and the **Ontario Arts Council** for our publishing program. We also acknowledge the financial support of the **Government of Canada** through the **Canada Book Fund** and **Livres Canada Books**, and the **Government of Ontario** through the **Ontario Book Publishing Tax Credit** and the **Ontario Media Development Corporation**.

Care has been taken to trace the ownership of copyright material used in this book. The author and the publisher welcome any information enabling them to rectify any references or credits in subsequent editions.

— *J. Kirk Howard, President*

The publisher is not responsible for websites or their content unless they are owned by the publisher.

Printed and bound in Canada.

VISIT US AT

Dundurn.com | @dundurnpress | Facebook.com/dundurnpress | Pinterest.com/dundurnpress

Dundurn
3 Church Street, Suite 500
Toronto, Ontario, Canada
M5E 1M2

For Arthur

CONTENTS

ACKNOWLEDGEMENTS

First, I would like to acknowledge the Supreme Court of Canada. Over the decades, the membership of this nine-person Court has altered through retirement (mandatory at age seventy-five) or death. Increasingly, the Court has tried to hand down judgments that come ever closer to being decisions that can be read, understood, and discussed by those who want to be informed about the structure of our law, of our government, and more importantly, of our society's values. So, I thank — most profusely — the Supreme Court of Canada.

A second link in the chain between the law and the people is the media. It is possible, of course, in our highly computerized society to read the decisions of the Supreme Court of Canada online, but that can be an arduous process. On occasion, magazines such as *Maclean's* feature a particular subject for investigative reporting, in which the Supreme Court of Canada's judgments (such as those relating to tobacco) may form a part. Newspapers such as the *Toronto Star* may select a story reflecting a matter of social concern, such as bullying. And, on a daily basis, radio or television may report on such stories.

The net effect of media reporting, at best, ranges from episodic to minimal. Perhaps the one constant to which I frequently refer in this series is the informed editorials in Canada's national newspaper, the *Globe and Mail*. Without hesitating, the *Globe and Mail* granted the right to reprint editorials (and there were many) on Supreme Court of Canada decisions. The approach of the *Globe and Mail* seems to be: Let the public be made aware. I thank them for their generosity and for maintaining consistently high standards.

I would also like to thank Penny Mallette and Michael Melgaard for their patience, thoughtfullness, and insight in bringing this series to fruition.

Ordinarily, I would say that I take full responsibility for the contents of this book. Hopefully, however, the contents do not reflect my judgments but those of the Supreme Court of Canada and, to a lesser extent, the lower courts. My task, as I saw it, was to discuss those judgments in a nonjudgmental and accessible way.

INTRODUCTION

Our bodies are ours to control, free from state interference. This principle seems enshrined in our Constitution through the Charter of Rights and Freedoms, and in the common law through which many of the Charter principles were nurtured. Section 7 of the Charter provides: "Everyone has the right to life, liberty and security of the person and the right not to be deprived thereof except in accordance with the principles of fundamental justice."

But, how absolute is this belief? Consider these questions:

- Do parents have the final decision in determining the medical care of their children — even if that choice may mean death?
- May children override the choices of their parents as to medical care? For example, if a teenager is pregnant and wants an abortion, may her choice override that of her parents?
- What role, if any, does the state (or the courts) have in reviewing individual medical choices?
- Are there laws against suicide or assisted suicide?

The questions address beliefs that can be deeply personal. A teenager has the strong religious belief that it is offensive to her god to receive blood transfusions no matter how sick she may be. Suppose she clings to that belief, which she shares with her parents. She suffers a disease that results in severe internal bleeding. If the teenager went to a hospital that operates under government rules, there is no doubt that the physicians would urge a blood transfusion — even against her wishes. If she stayed home, prayed, and hoped for a cure, she likely would die. If the police or child welfare agencies were not made aware of her situation, she would die. For government to act, it must first be made aware. (This, of course, does not preclude possible action after the event — for example, possible criminal action against the teenager's parents for failure to exercise parental duties in the proper care of their child.)

In the cases that will be discussed in the following chapters, bear in mind that the state, and eventually the courts, became involved in the "problem" only after it had been disclosed to them.

WHO ARE THE JUDGES?

A few words must be said about the judges (or justices, as Supreme Court of Canada judges are called). Who are they? How are they chosen? How do they go about coming to decisions? The answer to these questions may help us better understand the decisions that we will be examining.

In 1989 Beverley McLachlin, then chief justice of British Columbia, received a telephone call from the prime minister of Canada. He asked if she would consider a new position: that of a justice of the Supreme Court of Canada.

It was within the power of the prime minister, accepted by his Cabinet, to offer the position. The appointment of a justice of the Supreme Court of Canada did not have to go through parliamentary committee or parliamentary consent, as such — a process enormously different from that of the United States, where the president nominates and the Senate, following hearing, either gives the nomination a stamp of approval or rejection. (If the Senate rejects, then the candidacy of that person comes to an end.)

Justice McLachlin thanked the prime minister, accepted his offer, and became a justice of the Supreme Court of Canada. On January 7, 2000, the prime minister offered Justice McLachlin the position of chief justice of the Supreme Court, and she accepted.

There are nine justices who make up the Supreme Court of Canada. The conditions for their appointment are few, but they are important. They are appointed through the prime minister and the Governor in Council. In this regard, the "pool" for appointment by law is comprised of superior court judges or barristers with at least ten years in practice in a province or territory.

Once named to the Supreme Court, a justice cannot be removed from office so long as the justice carries out her/his duties in accordance with the law. But, at the age of seventy-five, there is forced retirement. (However, many retired justices are called back to serve in appointments such as chairing special commissions.) A serving justice can only be removed from office for bad conduct or incapacity (such as illness).

By law, the prime minister is required to appoint three justices from Quebec. By tradition, the prime minister also appoints three justices from Ontario, two from the West, and one from Atlantic Canada.

How the prime minister goes about selecting a justice for the Supreme Court, given the broad limits described, is for the prime minister to determine. In 2012 Prime Minister Stephen Harper set new guidelines. He named a panel of five members of the House of Commons: three Conservatives (the prime minister's governing party), one New Democrat, and one Liberal. Their task was to review a list of qualified candidates put forward by the federal justice minister in consultation with the prime minister, the chief justice of the Supreme Court of Canada, the chief justice of Quebec (where the next justice was to be selected), the Attorney General of Quebec, and provincial and territorial bar associations (as well as public suggestions).

The panel was instructed to submit a list of three recommended candidates — unranked — to the prime minister and he would select one from that list. A public hearing before a special parliamentary committee would be held before the prime minister finalized the appointment.

The first justice selected through the process described above was Richard Wagner, who was a long-time trial lawyer before becoming a justice of the Quebec Court of Appeal. In an interview with the *Globe and Mail*, Justice Wagner said: "I might surprise you, but I liked the [hearing] process. There is nothing to hide. I think a judge should follow the directions of society, and that means to explain to citizens what we do, how we do it and why we do it. I think it's fair and it's reasonable."

A central concern, said Justice Wagner, is ensuring access to the justice system for all Canadians.

SOME FACTS

On the whole, it can be said that justices of the Supreme Court of Canada historically do not like to talk about themselves. But, there are some facts that may give rise to questions going to the makeup of the Court:

- There have been no persons "of colour" appointed to the Supreme Court of Canada.
- There have been no persons from among the "first peoples" (First Nations, Métis, and Inuit) appointed to the Supreme Court of Canada.

The fact is that white men, drawn from an elite part of the legal profession, constituted the "pool" from which justices of the Supreme Court of Canada were drawn — at least until 1982. In that year — at the time the Charter of Rights and Freedoms, an important part of the Constitution of Canada, came into effect — the prime minister named the first woman to the Supreme Court: Bertha Wilson. She had immigrated to Canada with her husband John, a Presbyterian minister in Scotland, in 1949.

Justice Wilson had received an M.A. in philosophy at the University of Aberdeen. Once in Canada, she applied for admission to the law program at Dalhousie University in Halifax. She recalled an interview with the dean of the law school, and chuckled about it later. The dean advised her to "go home and take up crocheting." She didn't. She entered the Dalhousie law program in 1955 and was called to the Nova Scotia Bar after graduation.

In 1959 Justice Wilson moved to Toronto where she found employment with a leading law firm and later became head of research for that firm. Her job consisted in no small measure in writing opinions for members of the firm — a task that went a long way toward preparing her for work as a judge.

Justice Wilson received an invitation in 1979 to sit as a judge on the Ontario Court of Appeal. Her immediate response was surprise — and then laughter when, as a judge whose opinions reflected women's rights, she said: "I'll have to talk it over with my husband." She accepted the position on the Court of Appeal and served there until her appointment to the Supreme Court of Canada.

Justice Wilson was a Supreme Court justice from 1982 to 1991, retiring at the age of sixty-eight. There, she had an important role in interpreting the then newly established Charter of Rights and Freedoms, including decisions relating to a woman's right to abortion (*R. v. Morgentaler* [1988] 1 *Supreme Court of Canada Reports* 30) and a spouse's right to claim self-defence to murder based on physical abuse by her/his spouse (called in law the battered wife syndrome) (*R. v. Lavallée* [1990] 1 *Supreme Court of Canada Reports* 852).

Since the appointment of Justice Wilson, a number of women have served as justices of the Supreme Court of Canada. In 2012, after serving as a justice for what she called ten "intense" years, Justice Marie Deschamps of Quebec resigned at the age of fifty-nine. (At that time, there were four women sitting as justices.) In an interview with CBC News a week after her resignation, Justice

Deschamps was asked about "gender balance" on the Court. She answered, "I think every court should aim for half and half.... It's important that [the Court] is balanced.... I hope that the government will maintain at least four women on the Court. Whether the next candidate is a woman or it's the one that follows it will be for the government to decide."

In fact, the prime minister named Justice Richard Wagner of Quebec to the Court, thus lowering the number of women justices (at least for the time) to three.

It should be noted that the chief justice at the time of Justice Deschamps's resignation was Beverley McLachlin (CBC.ca, August 15, 2012).

HOW ARE JUDGES TO DECIDE?

May emotion play a role in decision-making? For us, in reviewing decisions of the Supreme Court of Canada (or the decisions of any court, for that matter), an important question is whether justices can decide a case largely on the facts and the law as given. Can they remove (or largely isolate) any individual bias?

There are two parts to the answer — at least as applied to the Supreme Court of Canada:

1. No single justice decides a case. If the Court sits as a panel, there usually are seven justices who meet, discuss, and work toward an opinion which the chief justice usually assigns to a specific justice. If there is disagreement that cannot be otherwise resolved, then the way is open to a written dissent or a concurring opinion. (Often the justices are able to work out their disagreement to form a majority or a unanimous opinion.)

2. A case may be one that summons enormous emotion. Such was the case of Robert Latimer, a Saskatchewan farmer

charged and convicted in the "mercy" killing of his disabled daughter. Twice the case went on appeal to the Supreme Court of Canada. The second time, the appeal was from a judgment of the Saskatchewan Court of Appeal that had increased a sentence of one year to ten years.

In a decision by the Court as a whole in the Latimer case — not one attributed to any particular justice — the Supreme Court of Canada affirmed the judgment. The role of emotion in coming to decision was lessened.

Justice Ian Binnie, on his retirement after serving fourteen years on the Court, commented on the Latimer case in an extensive interview with Kirk Makin of the *Globe and Mail*:

> The Robert Latimer case was a hugely controversial case, but to me, the legal outcome was straightforward. You can't have people making their own judgments as to whether their child should live or die.
>
> In saying that, I make no moral judgment about what Latimer did. I accept his word that he did it because he thought it was best for his daughter.
>
> But the legal decision wasn't his to make. But the law is clear. When you talk about judges applying the law and not making it up, if the Criminal Code is clear about the penalty that follows from the crime of homicide, then that is the penalty that follows. You can't apply the law differently from case to case depending on a judge's personal view of whether a constitutional exemption is warranted.
>
> So, there is no necessary [relation] between how much you agonize over a decision and what

the moral implications or the controversy is outside the courtroom. My only function in that case is the right legal result. In that case the legal result was clear. My personal views of whether it was a good outcome or a bad outcome were irrelevant (*Globe and Mail,* September 23, 2011).

REFERENCES AND FURTHER READING

Fitzpatrick, Meagan. "Supreme Court Should Have Four Women Says Retiring Justice." CBC.ca, August 15, 2012.

Makin, Kirk. "Justice Ian Binnie's Exit Interview." *Globe and Mail,* September 23, 2011.

_____. "Supreme Court Judge Warns of 'Dangerous' Flaws in the System." *Globe and Mail,* December 12, 2012.

CHAPTER 1
LET THE MEDICINE GO
DOWN – REGARDLESS?

What is a court's role in reviewing life-or-death medical decisions that affect the young? We are not speaking of decisions made by the parents of a young person. Rather, we are speaking of the decision by the young person, herself.

Of course, that decision can only be reviewed if authorities — often a hospital, or a doctor — become aware of it. It is possible for the young person to do nothing and to keep the illness to herself until it is too late for medical intervention.

The principal case discussed in this chapter is *A.C. v. Manitoba (Director of Child and Family Services)*, 2009, *Supreme Court of Canada Reports* 30, decided on June 26, 2009. A seven-member panel of Supreme Court of Canada justices set out three opinions that, in the result, allowed a hospital to administer blood to a critically ill fourteen-year-old (called A.C.) against her will. Without the blood transfusions, there was a real risk, based on medical evidence, that she might have died.

Justice Rosalie Abella spoke for the four-member majority, consisting of herself and Justices Louis LeBel, Marie Deschamps, and Louise Charron. Chief Justice Beverley McLachlin issued an opinion that concurred with the result reached by the majority. However, she would have reached that result primarily through an interpretation of the statute in question. She was joined by Justice Marshall Rothstein. Justice Ian Binnie was the sole dissenting judge. He would have allowed A.C. the right to refuse blood transfusions.

While the facts will be more fully set out, it is enough to say here that A.C.'s decision, in the view of the hospital's examining psychiatrists, was not made under duress or pressure of any kind, but that it reflected her sincerely held religious beliefs. And, in this regard, A.C. was fully aware of the possible outcome — namely, the possibility of death — if the hospital adhered to her wishes. After the transfusions, A.C. lived. The case was brought to the Supreme Court because A.C. argued that her personal rights had been violated.

Let us begin our overview of the case with principles in law. Medical procedures such as blood transfusions are, by their very nature, an assault on the recipient. A procedure may be designed for that person's well-being, but the underlying reality is beyond dispute: The doctor, the hospital, and those administering the procedure, are literally invading the body of the patient.

The common law — that is, the law developed by the courts over centuries — has within it certain values that are used to interpret statutes and, in that regard, individual rights and responsibilities. For example, there is the law of negligence, which, among other things, says that one cannot injure another without lawful right. And, if such a wrong occurs, then there may be a case for damages to the person wronged.

Many of the values of the common law have been taken, amplified, and written into statutes that control how government or its agencies may act on individuals. The most important of these basic laws is the Constitution, or, for our purposes here, the Charter of Rights and Freedoms. It is the highest law of the nation. However, it may appear that basic freedoms under the Charter may sometimes conflict with one another — even in matters involving life and death.

We will discuss these questions:

- Equality under the law is a fundamental freedom under the Charter. Yet, is it possible for there to be age discrimination in medical care? Can those under sixteen be denied the right to refuse medical care?
- To what extent may a court impose a maturity test in determining whether a young person may opt out of medical treatment?
- Freedom of religion is also a fundamental right protected by the Charter. Yet, may a court substitute the test of the "best interests" of the child to trump that person's firmly held religious convictions that compel her to refuse medical treatment?

First we will deal with the facts in *A.C. v. Manitoba (Director of Child and Family Services)*. Then, we will set out the opinions of the justices.

THE FACTS OF *A.C. v. MANITOBA (DIRECTOR OF CHILD AND FAMILY SERVICES)*

Two months before she entered the hospital, A.C. completed a written document called an "advance medical directive." It stated that she was to have no blood transfusions "under any circumstances," even if such transfusions meant saving her life. A.C. based this decision on her firmly held beliefs as a devout Jehovah's Witness. The Bible, she believed, imposed a mandate: No one was to take the blood of another. She had to follow that mandate, she said, if she were to stand "clean" with God. A.C. wrote: "I am one of Jehovah's Witnesses, and I make this directive out of obedience to commands in the Bible, such as: 'Keep abstaining ... from blood' (Acts 15:28, 29)."

But, saving her life was precisely what her doctor and the hospital medical team believed was the issue. They concluded that A.C. needed blood transfusions. She was experiencing bleeding from the bowel as a result of Crohn's disease, a chronic inflammation of the gastrointestinal tract.

According to A.C., her best interests were to be determined according to her religious convictions. However, the determination of the hospital — and, in the final analysis, the court — was that her best interests were to be measured by a standard based on what would likely protect her life.

We said this at the start of this chapter. Here, however, we go into more detail to better understand the issues and the Court's judgment.

The beginning point is to recognize A.C.'s age: She was fourteen years and ten months old. If she had been sixteen years old, under the Manitoba statute that controlled matters of medical consent, her wishes would have been determinative so long as she was rational and aware of the implications of that decision.

We will discuss the standard applied by the Supreme Court of Canada in passing on the extent to which A.C.'s wishes were to influence or control her medical treatment — even in the face of death. Now, however, our focus is how, in fact, the decision was made as to forced medication or, more particularly, blood transfusions.

Along with the decision of Justice Abella, who spoke for the Court majority, we draw on the description given by Justice Binnie, who was the lone dissenter in the seven-member panel of the Supreme Court of Canada that decided the case involving A.C. We do this not because there were variances on the facts between the justices whose views formed the majority opinion. Rather, it is simply because Justice Binnie had some additional details in his statement to which the other justices did not object. (Note: As a matter of practice, the justices generally exchange their opinions for comment or revision among their colleagues.)

A.C. ENTERS THE HOSPITAL

A.C. entered the hospital on April 12, 2006. The following day, her attending physician, Dr. Stanley Lipnowski, requested a psychiatric assessment of A.C. from the hospital's consulting psychiatrists. He wrote: "Please see 14 [year old female] admitted as [C]rohn's disease [with] lower GI bleeding. [Patient] is Jehovah's Witness refusing all blood product transfusions. Please do assess the patient to determine capability to understanding death. Thank you."

The assessment and report were completed that night between 10:00 p.m. and 11:45 p.m., during which time A.C.'s parents also were interviewed by the psychiatrists.

The potential of death was central to the inquiry. Three hospital psychiatrists — Dr. Kuzenko, Dr. Bristow, and Dr. Altman — examined A.C. and reported as follows:

> [Patient] is aware of medical concern for blood loss, [decreased hemoglobin] and that if blood loss is severe, a transfusion is the recommended [treatment]. She is aware of alternatives to transfusion - [erythropoietin] and iron. States that even if she will die, she will refuse blood based on scripture "to maintain a clean standing with God." She was voluntarily baptized two years ago and believes that "this is the absolute truth."
>
> Sleep is "pretty good." Concentration "good." Energy "really good." Eating well (apart from this past week).

The psychiatrists made inquiries to determine the extent of parental influence and reported:

> [A.C.] denies feeling pressured by parents and has a good relationship with them. Has good support system.

[The parents] believe she treasures her relationship with God and does not want to jeopardize it, that she understands her disease and what is happening.

The psychiatric assessment report concluded:

The patient appears to understand the nature of her Crohn's illness (and GI bleeding) and reason for admission. She also appears to understand the nature of her treatments, and that should her current medical status weaken, the treating MD's may suggest a blood transfusion. The patient understands the reason why a transfusion may be recommended, and the consequences of refusing to have a transfusion. At the time of our assessment, patient demonstrated a normal [mental status examination with] intact cognition (30/30 [Mini-Mental State Examination]).

At the time of her psychological assessment, A.C.'s condition was stable and continued to stabilize for a few days. She was being treated (with her consent) with non-blood products and medication to stop the internal bleeding. She had no desire to die, but she wished to live in accordance with her religious beliefs.

On the morning of April 16, she experienced more internal bleeding. Her doctors wanted to give her a blood transfusion, but she refused. Faced with that refusal, the hospital sought the intervention of Manitoba Child and Family Services. As a result, the director of Child and Family Services apprehended A.C. as a child in need of protection under the Manitoba Child and Family Services Act (CFSA).

"Apprehended" is a legal term used to describe taking control of A.C. and having the power to act in her "best interests" — a matter that, as we shall see, was finally determined by a court and not by A.C. or her parents.

A HOSPITAL/COURT HEARING: THE ORDER

The CFSA allowed the director to go to a provincial court and seek an order for the blood transfusions. But such an order could come only after a hearing and a finding by the judge of that court that the transfusions would be in the "best interests of the child." For this purpose, the CFSA defines a child as anyone under the age of sixteen.

If the child is sixteen or older, the court is forbidden to authorize examination or treatment without the child's consent. (This assumes, under the statute, that the child is able to understand the proposed procedure and its impact on her. Absent such understanding, a court may act in the child's best interests just as if the child were younger.)

The emergency CFSA application was heard by provincial Justice Morris Kaufman. Counsel for the director of Child and Family Services was in the courtroom. Others, including Dr. Lipnowski, counsel for the Winnipeg Regional Health Authority, counsel for A.C.'s parents, a social worker, and A.C.'s father, were together in a hospital boardroom and participated in the hearing by conference call. A.C. did not participate in the hearing.

Dr. Lipnowski's evidence was that the transfusions were necessary because the risk to A.C. if she did not receive blood was "significant." He stated: "[T]he longer she goes without [the blood transfusions], the more the risk is of her having serious oxygen deprivation to the point where [if] for argument sake she's not getting enough oxygen to her kidneys, they will shut down and cause essential poisoning of her system. If she does not get enough oxygen to her brain she can conceivably have seizures and other manifestations of the brain that will contribute to a faster demise or death."

Justice Kaufman allowed the blood transfusions over the child's objections. He concluded that when a child is less than sixteen years old "there are no legislated restrictions" on the court's ability to order medical treatment in the child's "best interests" under the CFSA.

To repeat, Justice Kaufman believed he had the right to order that which would be in the best interests of A.C. He was satisfied, based on the testimony of Dr. Lipnowski, that A.C. was "in immediate danger as the minutes go by, if not [of] death, then certainly serious damage."

Within hours, A.C. was given three units of blood. The treatments were successful and she recovered. On May 1, the director of Child and Family Services withdrew its application to apprehend A.C. At that point, there apparently was no medical emergency to be met.

THE LAW: APPLICATION TO APPREHEND

These are the provisions of the Manitoba Child and Family Services Act which Justice Kaufman interpreted in the case of A.C.:

§25(8). Subject to subsection (9), upon completion of a hearing, the court may authorize a medical examination or any medical or dental treatment that the court considers to be in the best interests of the child.

§25(9). The court shall not make an order under subsection (8) with respect to a child who is 16 years of age or older without the child's consent unless the court is satisfied that the child is unable:

(a) to understand the information that is relevant to making a decision to consent or not consent to the medical examination or the medical or dental treatment; or

(b) to appreciate the reasonably foreseeable consequences of making a decision to consent or not consent to the medical examination or the medical or dental treatment.

PROCEEDING BEFORE JUSTICE KAUFMAN

The following is a summary of the proceedings before Justice Kaufman as set out by Justice Binnie in his dissent in *A.C. v. Manitoba (Director of Child and Family Services)*. Note the additional detail.

At the §25 (CFSA) hearing, which proceeded in the absence of A.C., her attending physician, Dr. Lipnowksi, testified that because of reduced haemoglobin levels, A.C.'s vital organs were not receiving sufficient oxygen. Until her low haemoglobin level improved, the medical staff could not investigate by colonoscopy or [undertake any] other procedure [to determine] whether A.C.'s intestinal bleeding was continuing. While the non-blood medication presently being administered might assist in stopping further bleeding, it would not remedy the low haemoglobin count.

The risk to A.C. was significant even if the internal bleeding had stopped, because if the doctors waited for A.C.'s haemoglobin to rebuild naturally (i.e. without a blood transfusion), there could be permanent and serious damage to A.C.'s bone marrow and kidneys.

The CFSA hearing proceeded expeditiously. Counsel representing A.C.'s family, Mr. Allan Ludkiewicz, heard the evidence on behalf of the Director and Dr. Lipnowski over a cell phone on his way to the hospital. He urged the applications judge to come to the hospital as well to review the hospital's recently completed psychiatric assessment report, but the applications judge viewed such evidence as irrelevant in light of the language of §25 of the CFSA:

MR. LUDKIEWICZ [by telephone]: Yeah. I was going to request of the court that the, that the hearing be held at the hospital with — if, if My Lord would, would come down. I, I believe that the —

THE COURT [by telephone]: What's the, what's the purpose of that?

MR. LUDKIEWICZ: It's — what I understand is that this patient has been assessed as being capable of making her own decisions.

THE COURT: She's under 16.

MR. LUDKIEWICZ: She, she's been assessed by the doctors. There, there is an assessment report which I would want to put into evidence first and the assessment report indicates that [A.C.] understands the nature of her illness and the possible consequences.

THE COURT: Counsel, I — where — just help me out here. She's under 16. Is her consent required?

MR. LUDKIEWICZ: Her — if, if she's capable, My Lord.

THE COURT: Where does it say —

MR. LUDKIEWICZ: She's, she's in the same position as, as an adult. She makes her own medical decisions.

MR. THOMSON [Counsel for the Director]: Your Lordship, what the agency is relying on are the provisions of Section 25 of the Child and Family Services Act which clearly contemplate that *that type of investigation doesn't occur under the legislation for a child who is less than 16 years of age* and the provision that I would rely on in particular is subsection 9 of Section 25 of the Act [emphasis added].

MR. LUDKIEWICZ: Well, My Lord, first of all, the — this is a Charter matter, to begin with. I'd like to put that on the record. It involves Section 2(a) freedom of religion. It involves Section 7, liberty and security of the person. A capable person of any age makes their own decisions when it comes to, to health care. They have ... freedom of choice. So I believe that the first thing that My Lord should have before you is the assessment report.

The §25 hearing proceeded as soon as counsel representing A.C.'s family arrived at the hospital. The applications judge was conferenced in by telephone. Counsel again sought to introduce evidence as to A.C.'s capacity through the psychiatric report and through A.C.'s father, but was stopped by the applications judge:

MR. LUDKIEWICZ: In my examination of the father. When ... I was coming to this hearing, when I was driving it was indicated that we're assuming that [A.C.] has capacity; is that correct —

THE COURT: *I'm proceeding on the assumption that she has capacity and doesn't want this done. I'm taking that as a given* [emphasis added].

When counsel for the Director sought to ask A.C.'s doctor about A.C.'s capacity, the applications judge, consistently with his earlier ruling, did not allow it:

THE COURT: I think that if [A.C.'s capacity] becomes a live issue then I would want to attend and speak to the child myself and see the assessment report. But I am going to proceed, as I say. If we're going to proceed in this format then it seems to me only fair to proceed on the assumption that the child has capacity and that the child objects.

If I thought that, that [A.C.'s capacity] was going to be an issue, then I would deal with it by way of attending and speaking to the child and reading the assessment report rather than hearing Dr. Lipnowski's summary or opinion based on that, counsel. So I'm going to proceed without that [emphasis added].

Based on the attending doctor's evidence, the applications judge was satisfied that there was "immediate danger as the minutes go by, if not death, then certainly serious damage." He granted the treatment order because, in his opinion, §25(8) of the CFSA requires the court to act in what the court regards as the "best interests of the child" even for minors with capacity if they are under 16 years of age. In his view, the blood transfusion would be in A.C.'s best interests. He did not address the Charter issues. He issued an order:

"That qualified medical personnel are hereby authorized to administer blood transfusions and/or blood products to the Respondent [A.C.] as they deem medically necessary without the consent of Respondent [A.C.] or her parents."

A.C.'S APPEAL — THE FIRST STEP: MANITOBA COURT OF APPEAL

A.C. and her parents appealed Justice Kaufman's order:

1. They argued that section 25(8) of the CFSA, and the "best interests" test contained in it, applies only to minors under sixteen without capacity to make a mature medical decision. But, A.C. was determined to have had such capacity. Recall, this was assumed by Justice Kaufman and, on appeal to the Alberta Court of Appeal, that assumption was carried forward.

2. In any event, A.C. and her parents argued that sections 25(8) and 25(9) of the CFSA were unconstitutional because they violated the Charter of Rights and Freedoms, part of the Constitution of Canada and, as such, the highest law of the nation. The Charter overrules any conflicting statute. And, in this regard, they said that the questioned provisions of the CFSA unjustifiably infringed A.C.'s rights under sections 2(a), 7, and 15 of the Charter. Those sections provide:

2. Everyone has the following fundamental freedoms:
(a) freedom of conscience and religion;

...

7. Everyone has the right to life, liberty and security of the person and the right not to be deprived thereof except in accordance with the principles of fundamental justice.

...

15.(1) Every individual is equal before and under the law and has the right to the equal protection and equal benefit of the law without discrimination and, in particular, without discrimination based on race, national or ethnic origin, colour, religion, sex, age or mental or physical disability.

The Manitoba Court of Appeal rejected A.C.'s argument that section 25(8) of the CFSA applies only to children under sixteen without capacity. To have accepted that argument would have required the appellate court to read into the statute elements of the common law, that is, judge-made law, developed over the centuries. One such element is the rule relating to the *mature minor*. Aspects of this rule allow minors the right to make certain decisions — if they have demonstrated the maturity to be able to do so.

Rather, what the Manitoba Court of Appeal did was to look to CFSA itself. According to legal principles, courts are to interpret the law as written by the legislature, not the common law. The meaning of the law is to be found in the plain words of the law itself.

The court concluded that the legislation ousts the common law principles relating to mature minors and instead empowers the court to make treatment decisions for those under sixteen, with or without capacity, based on a "best interests" test. A child's wishes and capacity may be relevant to the analysis, but not determinative. The court stated that the Child and Family Services Act formed "a complete and exclusive code for dealing with refusal of medical treatment in circumstances where an application is made under §25 of the CFSA."

But what about the Charter? Were AC.'s rights under section 7 of the Charter violated as to life, liberty, and security of the person? Why should persons under sixteen be treated differently than those sixteen and older?

The Manitoba Court of Appeal identified the competing interests at stake as being the interest an adolescent has in his or her personal autonomy and, on the other hand, the state's interest in the protection of children and the sanctity of life. In the appellate court's view, section 25 of the CFSA successfully balanced these interests. It was not "arbitrary" to adopt the age of sixteen as the "presumptive line" because it cannot be said that the law "bears no relation to, or is inconsistent with, the objective that lies behind [it]."

CHALLENGE QUESTION

A REVIEW OF A.C.'S CAPACITY
TO DECIDE

To what extent did the lower courts — that is, Justice Kaufman and the Manitoba Court of Appeal — actually make findings as to A.C.'s capacity to decide as to the questioned blood transfusions? By "capacity" we mean maturity of judgment.

For purposes of decision, as noted, both Justice Kaufman and the Manitoba Court of Appeal assumed that A.C. had the maturity to decide as she did. Justice Abella, speaking for the majority of the Supreme Court of Canada in the A.C. case, stated:

No one in any of the proceedings determined whether A.C. was in fact able to
make a mature, independent judgment
about her medical treatment, and the psychiatric report was never subjected to a
review of any kind, let alone a searching
one.

Kaufman J. proceeded based on his
view that the question of A.C.'s capacity
was ultimately irrelevant under the Act,
concluding that when a child is under
16, there are no restrictions on the court's
ability to authorize medical treatment on
his or her behalf. At the Court of Appeal,
the question of A.C.'s capacity was not
even considered by the court. In response
to the Attorney General of Manitoba's
argument that the appeal should not be
heard because there was no proper evidentiary record of capacity, Steel J.A. [of the
Manitoba Court of Appeal] stated:

"I agree that the determination of
capacity is a delicate issue heavily dependent on the facts. *However, it is not
necessary to decide the issue of capacity
in order to address the legal issue raised
in this appeal.* The issue is strictly one of
statutory interpretation and, depending
on the meaning given to the legislation,
whether the legislation conforms with the
requirements of the Charter" [emphasis
added].

Since neither court in the prior proceedings assessed A.C's "best interests" in
light of her maturity, there is no reviewable
judicial determination before us as to A.C's
ability to make an independent, mature
decision to refuse the blood transfusions, in
accordance with the intense scrutiny con-
templated in these reasons for such circumstances. Moreover, the issue of the validity of
Kaufman J's treatment order is clearly moot
[no longer an issue that needs to be decided
by a court]. The medical emergency that
gave rise to this litigation is long since over
and A.C. is no longer under the age of 16.

WHY APPEAL?

Why would A.C. want to appeal the decision of the hospital and
Justice Kaufman after the blood transfusions had taken place? It
was matter of principle. A.C. and her parents believed that her
constitutional rights had been violated in an important way: She
was a minor, but she had rights under the Charter to have her
views factored into the final medical decision.

Though it wasn't discussed either by the Supreme Court of
Canada or the lower courts, the reality of the disease that brought
A.C. to the hospital was that the same symptoms might recur. A.C.
had Crohn's disease (regional ileitis). The disease can cause long-
term inflammation of part of the digestive tract (often the small
intestine). Its cause is unknown, but it is not believed to be heredi-
tary or infectious. The symptoms can include cramps and abdom-
inal pain. Severe bleeding that can cause iron-deficiency anemia

may occur. It is a disorder more common to the Western world, tending to strike those in their twenties. In about a quarter of the cases, the symptoms appear only a few times.

As noted, by the time the Supreme Court handed down its decision in the case of A.C., she had reached the age of sixteen. Under the Manitoba legislation, she had the right to make an enforceable medical decision denying blood transfusions — even to save her life — should another attack of Crohn's occur, assuming she otherwise understood the import of such a medical decision. (Justice Abella noted in her opinion that A.C. had reached the age of sixteen.)

THE SUPREME COURT OF CANADA DECIDES

The central issue before the Supreme Court in the A.C. case was whether the questioned provisions of the Child and Family Services Act (CFSA) were constitutional or, more specifically, whether they satisfied the requirements of the Charter of Rights and Freedoms. The answer to that question came in three opinions: the majority opinion given by Justice Abella; a concurring opinion of Chief Justice McLachlin; and a dissent of Justice Binnie. The basis for each of the three opinions was an interpretation of the CFSA.

A.C.'S ARGUMENT
Counsel for A.C. did not argue that CFSA was unconstitutional because it gave those sixteen and older the right to chose medical treatment or to reject such treatment — so long as they were competent. Rather, A.C. argued that the questioned provisions of the Charter had to be interpreted in a way that gave those under the age of sixteen the right to have their views as to medical treatment considered in decision-making.

Recall that the trial judge said he didn't have to consider A.C.'s views as to blood transfusions. He only had to consider what would be in her best interests.

Justice Abella wrote:

> The heart of A.C.'s constitutional argument is that there is, in essence, an irrebuttable presumption of incapacity in the Act for those under 16, and that this renders sections 25(8) and 25(9) of the Child and Family Services Act contrary to sections 2(a), 7 and 15 of the Charter.
>
> She does not challenge the constitutionality of a cut-off age of 16; she challenges the constitutionality of depriving those under 16 of an opportunity to prove that they too have sufficient maturity to direct the course of their medical treatment. Her submission is that at common law, mature minors, similar to adults, have the capacity to decide their own medical care. In failing to recognize this "deeply rooted" right, the statutory scheme, she argues, infringes the *Charter*.
>
> Her section 7 argument is that the provisions infringe her liberty and security interests and are contrary to the principles of fundamental justice because the inability of those under 16 to prove capacity is an arbitrary restriction. She argued that if the provisions were interpreted to include a rebuttable presumption that would allow her to lead evidence demonstrating that she had sufficient maturity to make treatment decisions, they would not be arbitrary and would be in accordance with the principles of fundamental justice.
>
> A.C. further argued that the provisions violate section 15 because they discriminate against

her based on age. Again, however, she concludes that if the legislation permitted her to demonstrate that she had sufficient decisional maturity, there is no discrimination.

Lastly, A.C.'s argument under section 2(a) is that the provisions violate her religious convictions as a Jehovah's Witness. Once again, it is her view that the ability to lead evidence of maturity would cure any constitutional infirmity.

THE MAJORITY APPROACH

Justice Abella, for the Court majority, turned to a number of interpretive tools to explain the meaning of the questioned sections of the Charter. By a considerable margin, at least judging from the space allotted to such tools, the legislative scheme itself and the common law have important places. (So it is that a number of exercises that follow focus on common law cases cited by Justice Abella.)

THE CFSA – LEGISLATIVE CORNERSTONE

First, however, let's examine what Justice Abella called the "legislative scheme" of the CFSA. This meant taking a look at the CFSA as a whole and asking how it impacts on the questioned provisions.

Justice Abella noted that the "cornerstone" of the CFSA is section 2(1)'s "best interests of the child standard." The Act then lists factors that go into determining the best interests of the child which Justice Abella listed, emphasizing certain portions:

(a) the child's opportunity to have a parent/child relationship as a wanted and needed member within a family structure;

(b) *the mental, emotional, physical and educational needs of the child and the appropriate care or treatment, or both, to meet such needs;*

(c) *the child's mental, emotional and physical stage of development;*

(d) the child's sense of continuity and need for permanency with the least possible disruption;

(e) the merits and the risks of any plan proposed by the agency that would be caring for the child compared with the merits and the risks of the child returning to or remaining within the family;

(f) *the views and preferences of the child where they can reasonably be ascertained;*

(g) the effect upon the child of any delay in the final disposition of the proceedings; and

(h) the child's cultural, linguistic, racial and *religious heritage.*

The CFSA defines a child as anyone under the "age of majority." In Manitoba, that age is eighteen (though for purposes of medical treatment, Manitoba gives any competent person sixteen or older the right to decide).

Importantly, Justice Abella noted:

In any proceeding under the Act, a child 12 years of age or more is entitled to be advised of the proceedings and of their possible implications for the child and shall be given an opportunity to make his or her views and preferences known to the decision-maker (§2(2)). Children under 12 can also have their views taken into account if a judge is satisfied that they are able to understand the nature of the proceedings and the judge "is of the opinion that it would not be harmful to the child" (§2(3)).

In summary then, for purposes of understanding the legislative scheme of the CFSA, it centres on the "best interests of the child." And it goes on to involve for those above the age of twelve the opportunity to input into medical decisions.

The chief justice would have confined her decision to an analysis of the CFSA itself; she would have reached the same conclusion as Justice Abella. However, Justice Abella believed it necessary to review other legal sources, especially the common law, for interpretive insights into the CFSA.

Justice Abella's summary of the common law began with the United Kingdom (where the common law first took root) and then moved to Canada. Her comparison of jurisdictions then went from the United States to and including Australia. She seemed to reach the following conclusions:

- The common law is not static. It has shown a capacity to reflect social changes. In this regard, the common law moved from denying minors (children) any input into medical decisions, and leaving such judgment to their parents or, in some instances, to the state itself, to a point where minors were permitted to make medical decisions so long as they were shown to have the maturity of a competent adult (what has been called the "mature minor" rule).
- Yet, even with this flexibility, parental authority does not end until the child reaches the age of majority. Rather, under the mature minor rule, such authority, Justice Abella said, recedes as the child grows older and approaches majority.
- The evolution of the common law often comes slowly, and then in response to individual fact situations. It is not like a law enacted by a legislature which might be addressed to a single problem.

THE GILLICK CASE

The first case from the United Kingdom cited by Justice Abella was *Gillick v. West Norfolk and Wisbech Area Health Authority*, 1985, 3 *All English Reports* 402. There, a doctor prescribed contraception for a girl under the age of sixteen without the permission of the girl's parents. The parents sued the doctor in tort (negligence) arguing that the doctor infringed on their parental rights (and duty).

The court majority stated that, under certain circumstances, a minor could consent to medical treatment without parental consent. Lord Fraser, for the court majority, said:

> It seems to me verging on the absurd to suggest that a girl or a boy aged 15 could not effectively consent, for example, to have a medical examination of some trivial injury to his body or even to have a broken arm set. Of course the consent of the parents should normally be asked, but they may not be immediately available.
>
> Provided the patient, whether a boy or a girl, is capable of understanding what is proposed, and of expressing his or her own wishes, I see no good reason for holding that he or she lacks the capacity to express them validly and effectively and to authorise the medical man to make the examination or give the treatment which he advises. After all, a minor under the age of 16 can, within certain limits, enter into a contract. He or she can also sue and be sued, and can give evidence on oath. Moreover, a girl under 16 can give sufficiently effective consent to sexual intercourse to lead to the legal result that the man involved does not commit the crime of rape.... Accordingly, I am not disposed to hold now, for the first time, that a girl aged less than 16 lacks the

power to give valid consent to contraceptive advice
or treatment, merely on account of her age.

Lord Fraser noted that a rigid legal line would fail to reflect
the reality that a child's transition from childhood to adulthood is
a continuous one. He said:

> It is, in my view, contrary to the ordinary expe-
> rience of mankind, at least in Western Europe in
> the present century, to say that a child or a young
> person remains in fact under the complete con-
> trol of his parents until he attains the definite age
> of majority, now 18 in the United Kingdom, and
> that on attaining that age he suddenly acquires
> independence. In practice, most wise parents
> relax their control gradually as the child develops
> and encourage him or her to become increasingly
> independent. Moreover, the degree of parental
> control actually exercised over a particular child
> does in practice vary considerably according to
> his understanding and intelligence and it would,
> in my opinion, be unrealistic for the courts not to
> recognise these facts.

But, what is it that the court "recognized"? Remember, as
Justice Abella pointed out, that the girl in *Gillick* had the advice
of a medical doctor in terms of contraception. She was not acting alone. There was a skilled professional — a physician — who
advised and whose advice she apparently accepted.

ANOTHER U.K. CASE CITED

It was several years after the *Gillick* decision that the English Court
of Appeal dealt with a more complicated case that, in its own way,

expanded the scope of the common law. At issue was a child's refusal of medical treatment "in the face of great injury or even death."

On the one hand, the court made it clear that it could override both the decision of parents and that of a mature minor. The court could act under an inherent authority as parent of the state (*parens patriae*) in the interest of the child. Yet, having said this, the court emphasized that the wishes and objections of the child "factor significantly" into the court's determination of the child's best interests. (This judgment is weighted in relation to the child's maturity.)

Lord Justice Balcombe stated:

> There is no overriding limitation to preclude the exercise by the court of its inherent jurisdiction and the matter becomes one for the exercise by the court of its discretion. Nevertheless the discretion is not to be exercised in a moral vacuum.... As children approach the age of majority, they are increasingly able to take their own decisions concerning their medical treatment.... Accordingly the older the child concerned the greater the weight the court should give to its wishes, certainly in the field of medical treatment. In a sense this is merely one aspect of the application of the test that the welfare of the child is the paramount consideration. It will normally be in the best interests of a child of sufficient age and understanding to make an informed decision that the court should respect its integrity as a human being and not lightly override its decision on such a personal matter as medical treatment, all the more so if that treatment is invasive.
>
> What I do stress is that the judge should approach the exercise of the discretion with a predilection [an initial view] to give effect to the

child's wishes on the basis that *prima facie* [on the
face of it] that will be in his or her best interests.

(The quote was included by Justice Abella in the A.C. decision.)
Lord Justice Nolan agreed. And, he stated that "in considering
the welfare of a child, the court must not only recognise but if necessary defend the right of the child, having sufficient understanding to take an informed decision, to make his or her own choice."

A MATTER OF COSTS

Usually, the party that wins in an appeal is awarded
court-determined costs — no small matter in an appeal case going
before the Supreme Court of Canada. However, A.C., in one sense,
did not "prevail." Her case was "moot" — that is, by the time of
the appeal, she no longer needed blood transfusions. Still, she won
the case in terms of the principle in question, namely, the right of
those under sixteen to have their views heard and considered in
medical procedures affecting them.

Justice Abella wrote for the Court majority:

> On the other hand, while A.C. has technically
> lost her constitutional challenge, she success-
> fully argued that the provisions should be inter-
> preted in a way that allows an adolescent under
> the age of 16 to demonstrate sufficient maturity
> to have a particular medical treatment decision
> respected. In these circumstances, it seems to me
> appropriate that since this is the major impact of
> these reasons, she should be awarded her costs.
>
> Accordingly, although the appeal from the
> Court of Appeal's finding of constitutionality is
> dismissed, A.C. is entitled to her costs throughout.

YOU BE THE JUDGE

AN ADULT IN HOSPITAL EMERGENCY

THE FACTS

Georgette Malette, a competent adult, arrived at an emergency room of a hospital unconscious. She was a Jehovah's Witness and carried with her a signed medical alert card clearly stating that no blood was to be administered to her under any circumstances. The attending doctor, acting on a belief in the sanctity of life, gave her a blood transfusion. He was aware of the medical alert card that she carried.

Malette brought an action against the doctor for battery — a common law claim for wrong done for which the remedy usually is damages (a money award). There is no doubt that the doctor acted in an emergency situation. Nor is there any doubt that the procedure used by the doctor (blood transfusion) was appropriate under the circumstances.

THE ISSUE

Even though the blood transfusion saved Malette's life, can the doctor be held liable for the wrong of battery?

POINTS TO CONSIDER

- Competent persons generally have the right to accept or reject any medical treatment.

- The signed card requesting that no blood transfusions be given was a clear expression of Malette's intention not to have any blood transfusions.
- The attending doctor, in ordering the blood transfusion, acted not only in good faith, but in the belief he was doing what the medical professions requires of him in protecting the life of a patient.
- The state has an interest in preserving the life and/or health of persons under its jurisdiction.
- Liability for battery in this fact situation is determined under the common law. There is no statute comparable to that involved in the case of A.C.

DISCUSSION

The facts reflect what Canadian courts have called a leading case — *Malette v. Shulman*, [1990], 72 *Ontario Reports* (2d series) 417 (Ontario Court of Appeal). There, the appellate court found the attending doctor liable for damages in battery.

Justice Sydney Robins, for the appellate court, explained the reasoning why, even when saving a person's life, a doctor must yield to a competent person's wishes. He stated:

A competent adult is generally entitled to reject a specific treatment or all treatment, or to select an alternate form of treatment, even if the decision may entail risks as serious as death and may appear mistaken in the eyes of the medical profession or of the community. Regardless of the doctor's opinion, it is the patient who has the final say on whether to undergo the treatment.... The doctrine of informed consent is plainly intended to ensure the freedom of individuals to make choices concerning their medical care.

To [give a blood transfusion to] a Jehovah's Witness in the face of her explicit instructions to the contrary would, in my opinion, violate her right to control her own body and show disrespect for the religious values by which she has chosen to live her life.

The state's interest in preserving the life or health of a competent patient must generally give way to the patient's stronger interest in directing the course of her own life.

In sum, it is my view that the principal interest asserted by Mrs. Malette in this case — the interest in the freedom to reject, or refuse to consent to, intrusions of her bodily integrity — outweighs the interest of the state in the preservation of life and health and the protection of the integrity of the medical profession. While the right to decline medical treatment is not absolute or unqualified, those state interests are not in themselves sufficiently

compelling to justify forcing a patient to
submit to nonconsensual invasions of her
person.

AN EXCEPTION TO THE RULE?

Suppose, however, that a patient arrives at a hospital emergency room unconscious and without a signed card, such as that carried by Malette. Attending doctors believe blood transfusions are necessary to save the patient's life, or at least to prevent significant physical harm. Would such action by physicians be treated as an exception to the decision in the Malette case?

The answer is *yes*. Justice Robins dealt with this fact situation in the Malette case. He stated:

> The emergency situation is an exception to the general rule requiring a patient's prior consent. When immediate medical treatment is necessary to save the life or preserve the health of a person who, by reason of unconsciousness or extreme illness, is incapable of either giving or withholding consent, the doctor may proceed without the patient's consent.
>
> The delivery of medical services is rendered lawful in such circumstances either on the rationale that the doctor has implied consent from the patient to give emergency aid or, more accurately in my view, on the rationale that the doctor is privileged by reason of necessity in giving the aid and is not to be held liable for so doing. *On either basis, in an emergency the law sets aside the*

requirement of consent on the assumption that the patient, as a reasonable person, would want emergency aid to be rendered if she were capable of giving instructions" [emphasis added].

NO MORE TREATMENT?

Jason and Robert had schizophrenia, a psychiatric illness. They were declared incompetent to consent to psychiatric treatment. Their physician wanted to treat them with neuroleptic drugs which, for many, control or minimize psychotic episodes or symptoms associated with schizophrenia. However, the drugs can have significant and unpredictable harmful side effects.

But before their psychiatric evaluation, Jason and Robert had made it clear that they did not want to take the recommended drugs in spite of their doctor's recommendation.

Should a court order the drug treatment? Justice Robins, speaking for the Ontario Court of Appeal, ruled that Jason and Robert (fictitious names) were to have their preferences respected (*Fleming v. Reid* [1991], 4 *Ontario Reports* (3d series) 74. His decision was based on an interpretation of the common law. He stated:

> *The right to determine what shall, or shall not, be done with one's own body, and to be free from non-consensual medical treatment, is a right deeply rooted in our common law.* This right underlies the doctrine of informed consent. With very limited exceptions, every person's body is considered inviolate and, accordingly, every competent adult has the right to be free from unwanted medical treatment. *The fact that serious risks or consequences may result from a refusal of medical treatment does not vitiate* [end] *the right of medical*

self-determination" [emphasis added by Justice Abella who quoted Justice Robins in *A.C.*].

YOU BE THE JUDGE

A CASE OF A "MATURE MINOR"?

THE FACTS

P.M. is a sixteen-year-old who is pregnant. She has consulted a physician and wants a therapeutic abortion. Her parents are aware of her pregnancy and have discussed it with her. They want her to have the baby. But it is also clear that P.M. is intent on an abortion.

There is every reason to believe that P.M. is healthy and that, with normal care, the pregnancy, if carried to term, would result in a healthy child. It is also clear that P.M. is what can be described as a normal and reasonably intelligent sixteen-year-old who simply does not want to mother a child at this point in her life.

For our purposes, we will assume that the pregnancy is in its first three months and that P.M. wants the abortion at the earliest possible time in order to avoid any complications — medical or emotional.

The hospital where the abortion would be performed has a special committee on abortions, and it has given approval to the procedure for P.M. The committee consists of physicians, surgeons, and a social worker. P.M.'s parents have brought an injunction (a court order to stop the abortion).

THE ISSUE

Does P.M. have the right to proceed with the abortion despite the wishes of her parents?

POINTS TO CONSIDER

- For our purposes, we will assume that the province where P.M. lives and where the abortion would take place does not have a statute similar to that of Manitoba, where A.C. lived. Rather, we will assume that the applicable law is that of the common law.
- The common law assumes that a "child" can be involved in the decision-making process relating to her health. The extent of that involvement — or her impact on decision-making — will be in direct relation to her maturity.
- In law, parents have authority or parental rights in relation to their child. Those rights continue until the child reaches the age of majority, or is otherwise "emancipated." (By "emancipated," we mean the child is no longer living at home and usually is self-supporting.)
- On the whole, in interpreting whether to allow such decisions by a child, a court will recognize child growth through adolescence.

DISCUSSION

The likelihood is that the injunction sought by P.M.'s parents will be denied. Justice Abella in *A.C.* cited a case with similar facts — *J.S.C. v. Wren* [1986], 76 *Alberta Reports* 115 (Court of Appeal). It was the reasoning in *Wren* that Justice Abella, speaking for the majority in *A.C.*, seemed to endorse.

That reasoning seemed to involve recognition that young people can grow to maturity and, as they do, that growth should be recognized and allowed to impact on decision-making. This is not to eliminate the role of parents in guiding children as they grow to maturity. Rather, it is, as stated, to recognize that such growth is a process — the result of which a court can recognize. This, in part, is what Justice Abella quoted from in the opinion of Justice Roger Kerans of the Alberta Court in the Wren case:

What is the application of the principle in this case? We infer from the circumstances detailed in argument here that this expectant mother and her parents had fully discussed the ethical issues involved and, most regrettably, disagreed. We cannot infer from that disagreement that this expectant mother did not have sufficient intelligence and understanding to make up her own mind. Meanwhile, it is conceded that she is a "normal intelligent 16 year old." We infer that she did have sufficient intelligence and understanding to make up her own mind and did so. At her

age and level of understanding, the law is
that she is to be permitted to do so.

Parental rights (and obligations) clearly
do exist and they do not wholly disappear
until the age of majority. The modern law,
however, is that the courts will exercise
increasing restraint in that regard as a child
grows to and through adolescence.

Justice Abella stated: "The proposition advanced in
Wren was not that a 'mature minor' was essentially an adult
for medical treatment purposes, but rather that courts must
give adolescents room to exercise their autonomy to the
extent that their maturity allows."

Perhaps. more to the point, Justice Abella did not have
to agree with the appellate court that J.S.C. was a mature
minor. It was enough for Justice Abella to recognize that
the common law had moved to the point of recognizing
that children, to the extent of their maturity, had a right to
be part of medical decisions affecting them.

RULES FOR CHILD MEDICAL INPUT UNDER THE CFSA

Justice Abella, speaking for the majority in *A.C.*, ruled that the
questioned provisions are to be interpreted in a way that allows
a child input into medical decisions in relation to that person's
maturity. The Court majority reached that decision having looked
at the Manitoba Child and Family Services Act (CFSA) as a whole,
and then having reviewed the common law, which, in a general
way (especially in the United Kingdom and Canada), seems to
have taken the same approach.

Yet, it remains to be seen how this generalization will be applied to facts. How is a court, as a practical matter, to determine whether and the extent to which it should allow, or balance, the judgment of a child against that of medical professional? Justice Abella, for the Court, attempted to provide some answers, though even they have a certain generality. Further, the listing provided is intended to aid, not necessarily to control, how decisions are to be made. This is what she said:

> In those most serious of cases, where a refusal of treatment carries a significant risk of death or permanent physical or mental impairment, a careful and comprehensive evaluation of the maturity of the adolescent will necessarily have to be undertaken to determine whether his or her decision is a genuinely independent one, reflecting a real understanding and appreciation of the decision and its potential consequences.
>
> As all of this demonstrates, the evolutionary and contextual character of maturity makes it difficult to define, let alone definitively identify. Yet the right of mature adolescents not to be unfairly deprived of their medical decision-making autonomy means that the assessment must be undertaken with respect and rigour. The following factors may be of assistance:
>
> • What is the nature, purpose and utility of the recommended medical treatment? What are the risks and benefits?
> • Does the adolescent demonstrate the intellectual capacity and sophistication to understand the information relevant to making the decision and to appreciate the potential consequences?

- Is there reason to believe that the adolescent's views are stable and a true reflection of his or her core values and beliefs?
- What is the potential impact of the adolescent's lifestyle, family relationships and broader social affiliations on his or her ability to exercise independent judgment?
- Are there any existing emotional or psychiatric vulnerabilities?
- Does the adolescent's illness or condition have an impact on his or her decision-making ability?
- Is there any relevant information from adults who know the adolescent, like teachers or doctors?
- This list is not intended to represent a formulaic approach. Its objective is to assist courts in assessing the extent to which a child's wishes reflect true, stable and independent choices.

How, it could be asked, would these considerations have applied to A.C.? Again, as a practical matter, A.C. was given blood transfusions against her will — and she lived. That deed cannot be taken back. If the transfusions had not been given, this much can be stated: The examining judge did not even seek A.C.'s input into the proposed procedure. If he had, it seems clear that the examining judge saw his duty as making a decision which would save A.C.'s life. In his view, so it seems, that was in the "best interests" of A.C. And, that was the statutory goal — deciding in a way that would favour A.C.'s best interests.

RESOLVING CONSTITUTIONAL ISSUES

Now, the question was whether allowing for growing input into decision-making by a person under sixteen comports with the

Charter. Justice Abella, again speaking for the Court majority in so ruling, wrote:

> Constitutional compliance in the context of the medical treatment decisions anticipated by §§ 25(8) and 25(9) [of the CFSA] means that the best interests standard must be interpreted in a way that is not arbitrary (to avoid violating section 7 of the Charter); not discriminatory on the basis of age (to avoid a section 15 violation); and not contrary to a child's right to freedom of religion protected by section 2(a). A.C. argued that all such constitutional violations can be avoided by allowing someone in her position to attempt to demonstrate sufficient maturity to have her treatment wishes respected.
>
> In my view, this is exactly what the "best interests" standard requires in medical treatment decision cases for adolescents. When the "best interests" standard is applied in a way that takes into increasingly serious account the young person's views in accordance with his or her maturity in a given treatment case, the legislative scheme created by §§ 25(8) and 25(9) of the Child and Family Services Act is neither arbitrary, discriminatory, nor violative of religious freedom.

Justice Abella then examined each of the rights claimed by A.C. under the Charter. In effect, by assuring those under sixteen the right to input into medical decision-making in relation to their maturity, their Charter rights are preserved. Here, we will go through each of the Charter rights claimed and Justice Abella's response.

1. Section 7 ("Everyone has the right to life, liberty and security of the person and the right not to be deprived thereof except in accordance with the principles of fundamental justice.")

Justice Abella stated:

> The inability of an adolescent to determine her own medical treatment ... constitutes a deprivation of liberty and security of the person, which must, to be constitutional, be in accordance with the principles of fundamental justice....
>
> A.C. argued that if the provisions are interpreted narrowly so that someone under 16 is deprived of the opportunity to demonstrate her capacity, they are arbitrary, and a law that is arbitrary will not be in accordance with the principles of fundamental justice.... A law will be arbitrary where it bears no relation to, or is inconsistent with, the objective that lies behind it. To determine whether this is the case, it is necessary to consider the state interest and societal concerns that the provision is meant to reflect....
>
> In order not to be arbitrary, the limit on life, liberty and security requires not only a theoretical connection between the limit and the legislative goal, but a real connection on the facts.... The question in every case is whether the measure is arbitrary in the sense of bearing no real relation to the goal and hence being manifestly unfair. The more serious the impingement on the person's liberty and security, the more clear must be the connection. Where the individual's very life may be at stake, the reasonable person would expect a

clear connection, in theory and in fact, between the measure that puts life at risk and the legislative goals.

It is therefore necessary to put the analysis into the context of the objectives of the provisions. The overarching goal of statutes such as the Child and Family Services Act is to protect children from harm.... In *B.(R.) v. Children's Aid Society of Metropolitan Toronto*, [1995] 1 *Supreme Court of Canada Reports* 315, La Forest J. discussed the importance of the state's role in protecting children:

The state's interest in legislating in matters affecting children has a long-standing history.... More particularly, the common law has long recognized the power of the state to intervene to protect children whose lives are in jeopardy and to promote their well-being.... *The protection of a child's right to life and to health, when it becomes necessary to do so, is a basic tenet of our legal system, and legislation to that end accords with the principles of fundamental justice, so long, of course, as it also meets the requirements of fair procedure* [emphasis added].

On the other hand, adolescents clearly have an interest in exercising their capacity for autonomous choice to the extent that their maturity allows. And society has a corresponding interest in nurturing children's potential for autonomy by according weight to their choices in a manner that is reflective of their evolving maturity. In order to promote this objective, paternalism should always be kept to a minimum and carefully justified.

Given these competing values, a problem arises when a child's interest in exercising his or her autonomy conflicts with society's legitimate interest in protecting him or her from harm....

Given the significance we attach to bodily integrity, it would be arbitrary to assume that no one under the age of 16 has capacity to make medical treatment decisions. It is not, however, arbitrary to give them the opportunity to prove that they have sufficient maturity to do so.

Interpreting the best interests standard so that a young person is afforded a degree of bodily autonomy and integrity commensurate with his or her maturity navigates the tension between an adolescent's increasing entitlement to autonomy as he or she matures and society's interest in ensuring that young people who are vulnerable are protected from harm. This brings the "best interests" standard in §25(8) in line with the evolution of the common law and with international principles, and therefore strikes what seems to me to be an appropriate balance between achieving the legislative protective goal while at the same time respecting the right of mature adolescents to participate meaningfully in decisions relating to their medical treatment. The balance is thus achieved between autonomy and protection, and the provisions are, accordingly, not arbitrary.

2. Section 15(1) ("Every individual is equal before and under the law and has the right to equal protection and equal benefit of the law without discrimination and, in particular, without discrimination based on race, national or ethnic origin, colour, religion, sex, age or mental or physical disability.")

There is no doubt that discrimination on the basis of age took place in relation to A.C. But Justice Abella ruled that it was not violative of section 15(1) of the Charter. She wrote:

> Under the Child and Family Services Act, the distinction between promoting autonomy and protecting welfare is presumed to collapse at age 16, subject to evidence to the contrary. But whether a child is under or over 16, the weight that is accorded to his or her views under s. 25 of the Act will ultimately correspond to a court's conclusions about the extent to which the child is capable of making decisions in his or her own best interests. By permitting adolescents under 16 to lead evidence of sufficient maturity to determine their medical choices, their ability to make treatment decisions is ultimately calibrated in accordance with maturity, not age, and no disadvantaging prejudice or stereotype based on age can be said to be engaged. There is therefore no violation of section 15.

3. Section 2(a) ("Everyone has the following fundamental freedoms — freedom of conscience and religion....")

A.C. made it clear that not taking a blood transfusion was important to her religious beliefs. She wanted her views taken into consideration by the examining judge. But the judge refused to do so. Again, A.C. wanted only to be listened to and have her views fairly weighed in the balance. Justice Abella agreed with this position. Decisions made in this way would not, she said, violate the Charter right to freedom of religion.

SUMMING UP

This is how Justice Abella summed up the majority decision:

> In conclusion, I agree with A.C. that it is inherently arbitrary to deprive an adolescent under the age of 16 of the opportunity to demonstrate sufficient maturity when he or she is under the care of the state. It is my view, however, that the "best interests" test referred to in §25(8) of the Act, properly interpreted, provides that a young person is entitled to a degree of decisional autonomy commensurate with his or her maturity.
>
> The result of this interpretation of §25(8) is that adolescents under 16 will have the right to demonstrate mature medical decisional capacity. This protects both the integrity of the statute and of the adolescent. It is also an interpretation that precludes a dissonance between the statutory provisions and the Charter, since it enables adolescents to participate meaningfully in medical treatment decisions in accordance with their maturity, creating a sliding scale of decision-making autonomy. This, in my view, reflects a proportionate response to the goal of protecting vulnerable young people from harm, while respecting the individuality and autonomy of those who are sufficiently mature to make a particular treatment decision.

WHAT IF?

Suppose a legislature gave courts an absolute right (unfettered discretion) to make medical decisions for children despite their actual capacities, while at the same time presuming that youths sixteen and over were competent to veto treatment they did not want.

Would such a law be valid under the Charter? Probably not. Justice Abella, herself, raised this question and answered it in the following way:

> If §§ 25(8) and 25(9) did in fact grant courts an unfettered discretion to make decisions on behalf of all children under 16, despite their actual capacities, while at the same time presuming that children 16 and over were competent to veto treatment they did not want, I would likely agree that the legislative scheme was arbitrary and discriminatory.
>
> A rigid statutory distinction that completely ignored the actual decision-making capabilities of children under a certain age would fail to reflect the realities of childhood and child development. However, this is not the effect of §§ 25(8) and 25(9) [of the CFSA]. As the foregoing analysis demonstrates, a child's maturity and corresponding interest in self-determination will factor significantly into any determination of his or her "best interests" under §25(8) of the Act, with the child's views becoming increasingly determinative as his or her maturity increases.

JUSTICE BINNIE DISSENTS

Justice Binnie of the Supreme Court of Canada dissented in the A.C. decision. [In his view, the trial judge (Justice Kaufman) still had the authority to make a final determination — even with A.C.'s input — that it would have been in her best interests for the blood transfusions to have taken place.] He had difficulty with the judge's finding of fact that A.C. had the maturity to make the medical decision refusing blood transfusions.

Justice Binnie stated:

> Children may generally (and correctly) be assumed to lack the requisite degree of capacity and maturity to make potentially life-defining decisions. It is this lack of capacity and maturity that provides the state with a legitimate interest in taking the decision-making power away from the young person and vesting it in a judge under the CFSA. Yet, this is not a case about broad government programs where line drawing and generalized age categories are sometimes essential and inevitable for administrative reasons. The CFSA requires individualized treatment decisions, and courts routinely handle capacity as a live issue under the CFSA in the case of minors between the ages of 16 and 18.
>
> The question here is whether in the course of those individualized CFSA treatment assessments the presumption of incapacity to refuse medical treatment can constitutionally be made irrebuttable in the case of young people under 16. I do not think it can. In such cases, the legitimate object and basis of state intervention in the life

of the young person has, by reason of the judge's finding of maturity, ceased to exist.

In short, §25 of the CFSA is unconstitutional because it prevents a person under 16 from establishing that she or he understands the medical condition and the consequences of refusing treatment, and should therefore have the right to refuse treatment whether or not the applications judge considers such refusal to be in the young person's best interests, just as is now the case with a "mature minor" who is 16 or 17 years old.

The Director argues that no Charter rights are absolute, which is true, but the onus is on the state to justify overriding an individual's fundamental choices about invasive medical treatment. We are not dealing with categories of people classified by age for administrative convenience as, for example, say, in the case of voting rights. The CFSA mandates an individualized assessment on a patient-by-patient basis.

In my opinion the deprivation of liberty or security of the person does not accord with the principles of fundamental justice where the only justification advanced for the deprivation, namely the incapacity of the young person, has been accepted by the applications judge not to exist.

REFERENCES AND FURTHER READING

* Cited by the Supreme Court of Canada.

Alderson, Priscilla. "Everyday and medical life choices: decision-making among 8- to 15-year-old school students." In

Children, Medicine and the Law, edited by Michael Freeman. Aldershot, UK: Ashgate, 2005.*

_____ . "In the genes or in the stars? Children's competence to consent." In *Children, Medicine and the Law,* edited by Michael Freeman. Aldershot, UK: Ashgate, 2005.*

Ambuel, Bruce and Julian Rappaport. "Developmental Trends in Adolescents' Psychological and Legal Competence to Consent to Abortion." *Law & Human Behaviour* 16 (1992): 129.*

"Blood Transfusion Case: Immaturity Is No Mere Stereotype." *Globe and Mail,* July 1, 2009.

Brazier, Margaret and Caroline Bridge. "Coercion or caring: analysing adolescent autonomy," In *Children, Medicine and the Law,* edited by Michael Freeman. Aldershot, UK: Ashgate, 2005.*

Bridge, Caroline. "Religious Beliefs and Teenage Refusal of Medical Treatment." *Modern Law Review* 62 (1999): 585.*

Buchanan, Allen E. and Dan W. Brock. *Deciding for Others: The Ethics of Surrogate Decision Making.* Cambridge: Cambridge University Press, 1989.*

Eekelaar, John. "White Coats or Flak Jackets? Doctors, Children and the Courts — Again." *Law Quarterly Review* 109 (1993): 182.*

Ferguson, Lucinda. "Trial by Proxy: How Section 15 of the Charter Removes Age from Adolescence." *Journal of Law and Equality* 4 (2005): 84.*

Fortin, Jane. *Children's Rights and the Developing Law,* 2nd ed. London: LexisNexis UK, 2003.*

Freeman, Michael. "Removing rights from adolescents." *Adoption & Fostering* 17 (1993): 14.*

Hartman, Rhonda Gay. "Coming of Age: Devising Legislation for Adolescent Decision-Making." *American Journal of Law and Medicine* 28 (2002): 409.*

Makin, Kirk. "Supreme Court to Hear Mature-Minor Rights Case." *Globe and Mail,* May 20, 2009.

_____. "Top Court Rules Transfusion Law Constitutional." *Globe and Mail,* June 26, 2009.

_____. "Top Court Gives Weight to Ill Children's Wishes." *Globe and Mail,* June 27, 2009.

Manitoba Law Reform Commission. *Minors' Consent to Health Care,* Report No. 91. Winnipeg: The Commission, 1995.*

Munby, Sir James. "Consent to Treatment: Children and the Incompetent Patient." In *Principles of Medical Law,* 2nd ed. edited by Andrew Grubb, assisted by Judith Laing. Oxford: Oxford University Press, 2004.*

Ross, Laurie Friedman. "Health Care Decisionmaking by Children: Is It in Their Best Interest?" In *Children, Medicine and the Law,* edited by Michael Freeman, Aldershot, UK: Ashgate, 2005.*

Sneiderman, Barney, John C. Irvine and Philip Osborne. "The Mature Minor Patient and the Refusal of Treatment." *Canadian Medical Law,* 3rd ed. Scarborough, ON: Carswell, 2003.*

"Teen Cannot Refuse Blood Transfusion, Top Court Rules." *National Post,* June 26, 2009.

Weithorn, Lois A. and Susan B. Campbell. "The Competency of Children and Adolescents to Make Informed Treatment Decisions." *Child Development* 53 (1982): 1589.*

CHAPTER 2

FORCED CONFINEMENT, FORCED MEDICATION

This chapter centres on persons who have been placed in psychiatric facilities because they are "not criminally responsible" (NCR) for crimes they have committed. The central questions raised are:

- What control, if any, do such persons have over the treatments their doctors think best for them?
- When and under what circumstances may they be released (discharged) from the institution?

Under Canada's Criminal Code, persons who commit criminal acts because of a mental disorder are not acquitted. They are not, as such, found innocent. Rather, because of their mental disorder, they are ruled not to understand the "nature or quality" of the wrong charged. They are not criminally responsible.

There is no presumption that an NCR individual is a danger to the safety of the public. On the contrary, the Criminal Code requires that persons found NCR be granted an absolute discharge (that is, released) unless a court or a review board is able to conclude that the individual poses a significant risk to the safety of the public. Even when this risk is established, the conditions for controlling the NCR individual are to be "the least onerous and least restrictive to the accused" consistent with the level of risk posed, ranging from detention "in custody in a hospital" to discharge "subject to such conditions as the court or review board considers appropriate."

Finding that an individual is NCR is not a finding of guilt. Nor is the detention of that person to be considered punishment. Rather, detention is required under the Criminal Code only for the purpose of protecting the public. Once that purpose has been served, then release is required. Moreover, as we shall see, any decision made by a review board or a court is not final. It is subject to regular and required review.

The Supreme Court of Canada has made it clear that the Charter of Rights and Freedoms requires no less. Among other rights, the Charter guarantees the life, liberty, and security of the person, except for those restraints which can be justified under principles of fundamental justice and in accordance with those reasonable limits accepted in a free and democratic society. Often, as in the cases discussed in this chapter, the principles of the Charter have been included in the statutes interpreted by the Supreme Court.

We will discuss two cases decided on the same day — June 6, 2003 — by the Supreme Court: *Dr. Russel Fleming v. Professor Scott Starson a.k.a. [also known as] Scott Jeffery Schutzman* and *The Queen v. Terry Steven Owen.*

In the Starson case, doctors attempted to compel medications that the patient refused on the ground that they would dull his brain and result in a life that for him would not be worth living. He was, however, willing to continue psychotherapy, and to voluntarily remain in the mental institution. The Supreme Court affirmed his right to refuse the medications.

In the Owen case, the NCR patient sought an absolute discharge from a psychiatric institution to which he had been committed more than eighteen years after he murdered a friend because of a drug habit that he could not or would not curtail. He argued that no psychiatric treatment (from medications to psychotherapy) would be of any benefit to him. Rather, he said that he should be released and, if he committed any other criminal wrong, then he should be punished just like any convicted person. The Supreme Court affirmed a finding that committed the patient to a mental institution. The Owen case will be set out in the "You Be the Judge" section.

Neither case involved the Charter as such. They related to: (1) the application of the statutes governing medications and restraining an NCR individual because of danger to public safety; or (2) the individual's ability to decide for himself whether to accept the medical care urged by doctors. The reason why the Charter was not brought into play seemed to be because the controlling statutes incorporated many of the relevant Charter rights. The Court's task was how to interpret and apply the statutes. We will deal first with the Starson case, and then proceed to the Owen case.

THE STARSON CASE: MEDICATIONS REFUSED

He preferred to be called Professor Starson. However, he was born Scott Jeffery Schutzman. At the time of the case before the Supreme Court, he was forty-seven. He was not by university training a professor. Rather, "professor" was an honorary title allowed him by many academics due to the quality of work that he had done in physics that, the majority of the Supreme Court said, was the "driving passion in his life."

His work centred on anti-gravity, the theory of relativity, and the measurement of time. He believed it was leading to the development of a starship — one that would allow for interstellar contact. He received some recognition among leading physicists. In 1991, he co-authored a paper — *Discrete Anti-Gravity* — with Pierre Noyes, professor emeritus of theoretic physics at Stanford University's

Linear Accelerator Center. Noyes described Starson's work as ten years ahead of its time. The publication date of the co-authored article may have some significance because it came eight years after Starson's perceived mental/sanity problems first arose.

The Supreme Court stated: "By all accounts, Professor Starson is an extraordinarily intelligent and unique individual." In fact, however, Starson's highest academic degree was that of an under-graduate in electronic engineering from Ryerson Polytechnic University in Toronto.

Schutzman changed his name to Starson in 1993, in part because (according to his mother, Jeanne Stevens) he saw himself as a son of the stars. He believed that he communicated with aliens from other planets. In interviews with reporters at the time his case came before the Supreme Court, he was said to have spoken "compellingly of his research and ideas for invention from per-sonal nuclear reactors to laser shavers." However, he also suggested to reporters that Pierre Elliott Trudeau, former prime minister of Canada, was killed by an alien; that Pope John Paul II worked for him; and that he had plans to marry comedienne Joan Rivers (whom he had never met). Starson saw himself as the world's greatest scientist, in addition to having world-class standing as a skier and arm-wrestler.

It was in 1983 that friends became aware of what they believed were Starson's mental problems. They found him in his Toronto apartment, huddled and delusional, in a large cage belonging to Mumbles, his blue macaw. Starson said that Mumbles was his son and the force of all intelligence in the universe. And, he had words about the Supreme Court (spoken before it sustained his right to refuse medications): "Your Supreme Court — and I mean no dis-respect by this — is Little League.... The Supreme Court does not have solutions. They report to me" (*Globe and Mail,* June 7, 2003).

Since that time, Starson had been in and out of a number of mental institutions. At times, he was placed in such institutions by order of a court, who found him to be not criminally responsible when he appeared on charges that he had made death threats against tenants in buildings in which he lived, and also against fellow employees. In no instance, as the Supreme Court noted, had Starson in fact injured or attempted to injure anyone, including himself — except in reacting against unwanted forced medication. It was Starson's refusal to take mind and mood-altering medications thought necessary by his attending physician at the hospital where he had been admitted as an NCR patient that gave rise to the case before the Supreme Court.

Psychiatrists had diagnosed Starson as likely suffering from what is medically called a bipolar affective disorder. For him, the disorder had elements of schizophrenia and manic depression. It can give rise to sudden behavioral outbursts and delusions. Some psychiatrists said that if his condition was left untreated by medications, it would worsen. Indeed, they already believed that this had happened to Starson and that his condition might be called psychotic. Other psychiatrists stated that there simply was no proof that medications would slow or stop any worsening condition.

Starson's mother, whom he had chosen not to see for more than a year before his case was heard, wanted her son to be on the medications recommended by his physicians — even if they had to be forced. She said: "When medicated, he's the most charming, fascinating, nice individual.... [Without medication] he can't keep a thought going in a straight line for one minute."

The death threats made by Starson, which resulted in his NCR status, really were more of a risk to Starson, himself, than to the recipients, his mother seemed to imply: "He is provocative to other people. Not everybody will put up with it. He has been assaulted many times before, and I'm afraid someone will kill him. He is a menace to society. He is his own worst enemy." Of the Supreme Court's decision, she said: "I don't think what they did was a humane judgment.... It's a disaster because they have destroyed his life and his dream.... It's the end of his life."

The Schizophrenia Society of Canada, an advocacy group which the Court allowed to intervene, argued: "The very part of your brain that makes rational decisions is the part of you that's ill." In effect, the Society stated that Starson, because of the nature of his illness, simply was not able to make a rational decision as to whether to take the medications his doctors recommended.

WHAT STARSON UNDERSTOOD

Starson, at the time of the case, lived in the medium-security forensic psychiatric unit at the Royal Ottawa Mental Health Centre. It was a secure ward. There were no regular visiting privileges. But, said Starson, "It's better than where I was."

At one point in his stay at mental institutions, Starson accepted medications that he said left him incapacitated and drooling. Those medications, his doctors stated, were different from the drugs they urged should be forcibly given to Starson. However, in an interview with the *Canadian Press* a year before the Court's decision, Starson said: "I completely, cognizantly got myself into this. I knew I was making a choice I couldn't go back on" (*Canadian Press*, June 6, 2003).

Justice John Major, who gave the opinion for the Supreme Court majority in *Starson*, summarized the record as to Starson's understanding of his mental condition and the possibilities (and limits) of the proposed treatments: "Professor Starson acknowledged that he suffered from a mental condition, and appreciated the purpose of the proposed medication and the possible benefits suggested by the doctors. He had tried other treatments in the past to no avail. The evidence did not suggest that enforced treatment was likely to improve his condition."

In saying this, Justice Major quoted from Starson's testimony before the trial tribunal. There, Starson both accepted that he had mental problems and that he showed symptoms of what psychiatrists call bipolar disorder, though he did not equate his "problems" with mental illness. Rather, he was of the view that through psychotherapy he could resolve his problems. And, until that time, he voluntarily would stay in the mental institution. But, he stated, the stay would not likely be lengthy:

> I certainly have exhibited the symptoms of these labels that you give [as to bipolar disorder]. [For example] manic is a fairly clear label. And certainly I have exhibited things that would be considered manic....
>
> I had mental problems thirteen years ago that were difficult, almost impossible for me to handle. What I differ on is that the cause of these problems was not a mental illness.... You [psychiatrists] are a religion. I have the perfect scientific mind. Only you people say I have an illness. [But, these problems which I have] have not been resolved.... However, [through psychotherapy with a hospital psychiatrist, Dr. Posner,] I will learn how to deal with [these problems].... I will be able to go back to [my] life even better than it was before.

Starson made it clear that his perception of reality differed from that held by many others.

WHAT THE ATTENDING PSYCHIATRISTS UNDERSTOOD

Dr. Paul Posner was the psychiatrist upon whom Starson apparently placed some hope that, through psychotherapy, there would be recovery. Dr. Posner, who said that he also was the recipient of a death threat from Starson, in fact offered little promise. He said that Starson simply lacks the mental ability to consent to medical treatment:

I feel [Professor Starson] is not capable to make consent — to make treatment decisions on his own behalf in any way, shape or form. Professor Starson cannot even be engaged in a discussion of a mental illness as it pertains to him. He can't be engaged in the use of medications as they pertain to him.... [A]ll of the above virtually rules out discussing the consequences or appreciating the consequences of not taking medications....

[D]espite the fact that he may be able to reiterate and he's got a good memory ... I don't believe that he has any appreciation whatsoever of what those side-effects could mean in terms of him. And I don't think he has the ability to engage in a discussion of any sort that would allow him to become more knowledgeable in that area. I mean, at least to argue on a rational basis. No, I don't think he could do that. So I don't think he meets any of the sort of criteria for capability of making treatment decisions and I don't think he's — I don't even think he's close on any of them....

I can say that none of that intelligence [in physics] bears any — has any role in his understanding — has not contributed to his understanding of mental illness. In fact, in an indirect way, all that intelligence may be reinforcing his delusional system. He may be using it to perpetuate things. Maybe at a faster or more impressive rate than the average delusional patient.

One of the things about delusions is that when you develop these kinds of illnesses, you can't effectively evaluate what happens around you, so you begin to construct your own reality.

Sometimes you borrow it from the Bible, from science fiction, from whatever source. Sometimes, especially if you're smart enough, if you've got enough raw intelligence, you build it yourself, perhaps on a skeleton of something else. And I think that's where the intelligence has gone. I don't think it's certainly gone into understanding that he has a mental illness....

I don't agree that [Professor Starson's] disorder has been a steady psychotic state. In fact, it's been a progressive psychotic state and there are a lot of very good pieces of evidence to support that.... What [this death threat to a hospital worker] means to me is that the illness has taken on another dimension. If provocation of ... that objectively small or innocent of a degree could have evoked that kind of explosion, that concerns me, because ten or fifteen years ago, I don't believe it would have [happened]....

[T]he literature from bipolar disorder shows that untreated ... mania ... can and often does progress in severity, so it's not a question of maintaining the status quo. If you sit still and do nothing, harm will happen at a physiologic level, evidenced by the worsening of his state, as perceived by others.

Dr. Ian Swayze, a second psychiatrist at the institution where Starson was held, said that Starson was not capable of giving his consent. He said that Starson was not able to understand the foreseeable consequences of refusing the treatment proposed and, in that regard, that he was unable to understand the information necessary to making an informed decision. Dr. Swayze offered this example:

We [Dr. Swayze and Starson] then attempted to review, or I attempted to review, the risks and benefits of those medications and was, once again, quickly interrupted: All chemicals are rejected [said Starson], with the understanding by myself that that inferred that there were no medications which were amenable or appropriate for a bipolar disorder or psychotic episodes and that there was no consideration that those [medications] would be appropriate under any circumstances.

I've attempted to focus on the issue of the benefit of those medications. "None exist," [Starson said]. Then [I tried to] canvass the area of risk involved in rejecting medications and was told [by Starson], in no uncertain terms, once again, that the medications were chemicals. They should be rejected and that there was no risk of rejecting them, as they would, in fact, inflict injury upon any person foolish enough to accept them.

THE LEGAL CONTEXT FOR "FORCED" CONSENT
Starson's doctors had no legal right to force drugs upon him even if they thought (as they did) that such treatments would be in his best interest. The reasons, based on important values recognized in Canadian law, were stated by Chief Justice McLachlin in her dissent in the Starson case. Her view, in that regard, also reflected the majority decision of Justice Major.

The individual is to be respected as such in law. The individual, so long as he/she has the capacity to decide, must be afforded that right despite good medical opinion to the contrary. And, though neither the chief justice nor Justice Major said so expressly, they impliedly referred to the constitutional basis for that right, found in the Charter of Rights and Freedoms. For example, section 7 of the Charter provides: "Everyone has the right to life, liberty and security of the person and the right not to be deprived thereof except in accordance with the principles of fundamental justice."

The chief justice, again agreeing with the majority in *Starson*, stated:

> Ordinarily at law, the value of autonomy prevails over the value of effective medical treatment. No matter how ill a person, no matter how likely deterioration or death, it is for that person and that person alone to decide whether to accept a proposed medical treatment.
>
> However, where the individual is incompetent, or lacks the capacity, to make the decision, the law may override his or her wishes and order hospitalization. For example, young children generally lack capacity to make medical decisions because of their age. Thus their parents or guardians, not they, decide what medical treatment they should receive. Where mental illness deprives a person of the ability to make a decision about medical treatment, the law may permit that person's wishes to be overridden.

With the Charter rights mentioned looming in the background, provinces such as Ontario, through their legislatures, have drawn lines for determining capacity to consent for medical treatment (Health Care Consent Act, 1996 [HCCA], *Statutes of Ontario* 1996, Chapter 2, Schedule A).

Starson's doctors wanted to treat his bipolar disorder with a number of medications, including neuroleptics, mood stabilizers, and anti-anxiety and anti-parkinsonian drugs. This was a different range of medications than Starson earlier had allowed. Those earlier medications had reduced his delusions, but they also had side effects that Starson thought were unbearable: They dulled his brain. The new medications, his doctors said, promised better results with "reduced negative side effects." The doctors said that Starson's condition would grow worse without the proposed treatments.

Starson refused medications of any kind. He would only agree to psychotherapy. He went before the Consent and Capacity Board (CCB) — composed of a psychiatrist, a lawyer, and a lay person — set up under the HCCA. He asked the board to rule that, within the meaning of the HCCA, he was capable of refusing treatment.

Basing their reasoning on the views of Starson's attending psychiatrists, the CCB found that Starson was not capable. It gave little weight to his testimony or that of friends and colleagues that contradicted the evidence of the psychiatrists. The Board stated that, in its opinion, Starson was in "almost total denial" of his illness.

It was the Board's view that without an acknowledgment of his illness, Starson could not relate information to his own particular disorder, and therefore could not understand the consequences of either refusing or consenting to medication. Further, the Board found that he did not "appreciate the risks and benefits of a treatment decision."

The benefits, as the Board saw them, were that "the medications would bring an improvement in Starson's delusional state ... and a possible resumption of his goals in the scientific field."

Starson therefore was, in the Board's view, "incapacitated." This meant that if the board's decision were upheld, he could have been forcibly medicated — that is, injected with the medications that the psychiatrists thought necessary but that Starson argued would condemn him to a life he did not want to lead.

However, under the HCCA, Starson appealed to the Ontario Superior Court, which had the power to reverse the Board's findings if it determined them to be "unreasonable." And, that is what the judge did. She ruled that Starson did not deny his illness. Further, the Board had failed to consider the extent to which his illness and claimed delusions affected his ability to understand information his doctors gave him, or the consequences flowing from the treatments they proposed. And, the Board, in the final analysis, had acted not on objective evidence, but on the subjective basis of what it believed to be the "best interests" of Starson.

Two years later, in 2001, the Ontario Court of Appeal heard and handed down its unanimous decision affirming the judgment of the Superior Court:

1. It agreed that Starson was aware that he had "mental problems."
2. There was no evidence from the doctors that any of the medications given to Starson had helped him.
3. More importantly, Starson's refusal to take the proposed medications was based on the harmful effects they might have on his scientific work. Yet, the Court of Appeal acknowledged that Starson's refusal, objectively, might well not be in his best interests.

MENTAL ILLNESS AND INCAPACITY

Suppose an individual is found to be seriously mentally ill. Does it follow that this person lacks the capacity to make decisions concerning his/her medical treatment, including that relating to mental health? As to this question, both the dissent and the majority in *Starson* were in agreement that the answer was *no*. For example, the chief justice stated: "[But] mental illness is not conflated [to be fused] with incapacity. Mental illness without more does not remove capacity and autonomy. Only where it can be shown that a person is unable to understand relevant factors and appreciate the reasonably foreseeable consequences of a decision or lack of decision can treatment be imposed."

It also follows, the chief justice said, that merely because a mentally ill person has a fine intellect, there is not necessarily legal capacity.

A FAST-TRACK DECISION?

An important aim of the Health Care Consent Act is to speed treatment for incapable patients. This is done by putting time limits on the Consent and Capacity Board (CCB) to which Starson appealed. Within seven days of receiving an application appealing forced medication, the Board must have a hearing. And it must hand down a decision within one day from the end of that hearing. If a party asks for reasons for the Board's decision, they must be provided with such reasons within two (business) days of the request.

There may have been required speed on the part of the CCB, and some limitation on the Superior Court in terms of the extent to which it was able to review the board's findings. But, from the time the board and the Superior Court handed down their decisions in 1999, two years passed before the Ontario Court of Appeal decided the matter, and another two years passed before the Supreme Court handed down its decision.

BURDEN OF PROOF

Who had the burden of proof to show that Starson had the "capacity" to accept or reject medical treatment? The burden of proof is on the attending physician(s) to demonstrate that Starson is incapable, within the meaning of the law, to make the decision as to treatment. In this regard, the law presumes that Starson is capable to decide to reject or accept the proposed medical treatment. Whether this burden has been carried is determined by looking at the evidence in terms of the "balance of probabilities."

THE SUPREME COURT DECIDES

In a 6–3 decision, the Supreme Court affirmed the judgment of the Ontario Court of Appeal. Starson was found to have the capacity to refuse the medical treatment urged by his doctors. Justice Major handed down the majority judgment and Chief Justice McLachlin spoke for the dissenting justices. We will deal first with the majority decision.

CAPACITY

The central question in *Starson* was whether, under the Health Care Consent Act, Starson had the capacity to decide whether to accept the medical treatments recommended by his psychiatrists. In this regard, all members of the Court emphasized that Starson's capacity to decide could be quite different from whether he had a mental illness.

Capacity, said Justice Major for the Court majority, is defined by the HCCA: "A person is capable with respect to a treatment [or] admission to a care facility ... if the person is able to understand the information that is relevant to making a decision about the treatment, [or] admission ... as the case may be, and able to appreciate the reasonably foreseeable consequences of a decision or lack of decision."

There are two elements to this definition, Justice Major stated:

1. A person must be able to understand the information relevant to making a treatment decision. This means the objective ability to "process, retain and understand the relevant information." Justice Major found that there was "no doubt" that Starson met this condition.
2. A person must be able to "appreciate the reasonable foreseeable consequences" of the decision taken. This means that the patient must be able to apply the relevant information to his or her situation, and be able to weigh the foreseeable risks

and benefits of the decision made. Here, the CCB had found Starson lacking.

The Board's analysis was in two parts: (1) the benefits of treatment, and (2) the risks of non-treatment.

BENEFITS OF TREATMENT

The CCB found that Starson failed to appreciate the likely benefits of treatment which it defined as "improvement in his delusional state ... and a possible resumption of his goals in the scientific field."

On review, the Superior Court (the lower court) said that it was one matter to accept the Board's findings if they were supported by some evidence in the record. Here, however, the Superior Court judge ruled, there was no evidence that the proposed treatments would help Starson's condition:

> There was no evidence that the proposed medication was likely to ameliorate [help] Professor Starson's condition. Dr. Swayze [one of Starson's attending psychiatrists] testified that it was "unclear" whether treatment would facilitate a "normal functioning level," and that treatment in the past had never enabled Professor Starson to function adequately. Dr. Posner [another of Starson's psychiatrists] noted that, in general, only 60 percent of patients treated with neuroleptics [one of the proposed medications] respond favourably to new treatment.
>
> The evidence does not suggest that Professor Starson would fall into that category. [He] stated that medication attempts "have always been the most horrible experiences of my life." The end goal of the proposed treatment was to place

Professor Starson on mood stabilizers. Both Professor Starson and Dr. Swayze confirmed that he had tried different mood stabilizers in the past. Starson testified that he had "been through all the treatment [and] it hasn't worked."

Furthermore, Professor Starson appreciated the intended effects of the medication: "I've been through these chemicals that they propose before – and I know the effects and what they want to achieve is slow down my brain, basically...." The attending physician agreed that the purpose of the medication was to slow down Professor Starson's brain to a normal range.

[The attending physician stated:] "If by that he refers to slowing down speech, or racing thoughts, or intrusive thoughts, which would be characteristic elements in a manic episode, then that is my intention. If it is to blunt him beyond what would be put [at] a normal range of mood and thought process without psychosis, then that is my intent."

[Starson's] stated position on medication was that "should the individual think the medications are helping them, by all means then the individual should be on the medications." As noted, however, his past experience led him to believe that the medication would not help him. Although Professor Starson did not believe the medication would affect his sense of reality, there was no clear evidence, as the reviewing judge [of the Ontario Superior Court] observed, with respect to the nature and extent of Professor Starson's delusions or "as to what delusions the medication would eliminate or control."

Most importantly, Justice Major said, the CCB failed to understand Starson's underlying reasons, which he stated, for refusing medication. Starson did not want to be "normal," at least as he believed that term was defined by his psychiatrists. And, it was this failure which was central to the majority decision of Justice Major, who wrote:

> Professor Starson stated that the medication's normalizing effect "would be worse than death for me, because I have always considered normal to be a term so boring it would be like death." The evidence indicates that the dulling effects of medication transformed Professor Starson "into a struggling-to-think drunk," a result that precluded him from pursuing scientific research. Professor Starson stated unequivocally that every drug he had previously tried had hampered his thinking. As a result, there was no basis for the Board to find that a possible benefit of treatment would be the resumption of his work as a physicist. The evidence, in fact, suggests just the opposite. It is apparent from the record that Professor Starson values his ability to work as a physicist above all other factors. It is clear that he views the cure proposed by his physicians as more damaging than his disorder.

RISKS OF NON-TREATMENT

The CCB found that Starson did not appreciate the risks that would follow from refusing the medications: His mental disorder would worsen. This, too, was a finding of fact. On the whole, the Superior Court would accept that finding if there were a reasonable basis in the record for doing so. The Superior Court ruled that there was no such basis.

It is true, the court stated, that both of Starson's psychiatrists — Dr. Swayze and Dr. Posner — concluded that Starson's mental condition either would continue to worsen or had already worsened beyond the point of possible treatment. But these were conclusions, said the court, without any substantial evidentiary base.

Dr. Swayze, for his part, referred to Starson's previous hospitalizations, which he said "suggest a chronic, unremitting course." Dr. Posner referred to medical literature which indicated that "untreated mania can and often does progress in severity." He noted, too, that Starson had not published any academic articles in "three or four years" before the CCB hearing. And, in conversations with other psychiatrists at the institution, he concluded that Starson was relatively more irritable than in the past.

Justice Major, for the Supreme Court, stated:

> Putting aside this scant evidentiary basis, Professor Starson was never asked at the hearing whether he understood the possibility that his condition could worsen without treatment. The presumption, of course, is that a patient has the ability to appreciate the consequences of a treatment decision. The onus [burden of proof] is not on Professor Starson to prove this ability.
>
> As noted ... Professor Starson was alert to the presence of a mental condition and the need to be in hospital to treat that condition. In light of his awareness of the need for treatment, it was unreasonable for the Board to conclude, without further inquiry, that [Starson] failed to appreciate the possibility that his condition could worsen.
>
> In summary, there was no basis to find that Professor Starson lacked awareness of his condition or that he failed to appreciate the consequences of treatment. In the absence of these

findings, there was no support for the Board's ultimate finding of incapacity. As a result, Molloy J. [of the Ontario Superior Court] correctly set aside the Board's decision.

THE DISSENT

Chief Justice McLachlin agreed with a number of points made by the majority. Her dissent, joined by Justices Charles Gonthier and Louis LeBel, summarized the differences, as she saw them:

> On the facts, my colleague Major J. and I agree that there was evidence that Professor Starson suffered from serious mental illness; that he accepted he had symptoms of mental illness which had created difficulties for him in the past and for which he was prepared to accept psychotherapy; that he did not agree with his physicians on the diagnosis of this illness; and that without the proposed medical treatment, he might continue to deteriorate. We also agree that Professor Starson did not wish to accept the proposed medication-based therapy because of the effects of previous drug therapy, in particular the fact that it dulled his intellectual functioning.
>
> On the law, my colleague and I agree that it would be erroneous for a [Consent and Capacity] Board to find incapacity simply because the patient does not accept the doctors' diagnosis or because treatment is in the best interests of the patient.
>
> The central differences between my colleague [Justice Major] and me appear to be two: whether there was evidence to support the Board's

conclusion on capacity; and whether the Board erroneously applied a best interests standard.

In my respectful view, the evidence amply supports the Board's findings of Professor Starson's inability to understand the information relevant to treatment and to appreciate the reasonably foreseeable consequences of a decision or lack of decision. Nor, in my view, did the Board erroneously apply a best interests standard. Rather, it remained focused on the question of capacity throughout. Given this evidence and the Board's application of the correct legal tests, I see no basis upon which a court of judicial review can set aside its decision.

For the Court majority, Justice Major made this comment on the dissent:

I disagree with the conclusion of my colleague, McLachlin C.J. Her reasons, with respect, appear to disregard the bulk of Professor Starson's testimony. Absent is the candid acknowledgement by him of his mental problems, his obvious appreciation of the intended purpose of the medication, the admitted uncertainty by the doctors that treatment would improve Professor Starson, the failure in the past of mood stabilizers, which was the end goal of the proposed treatment ... and his rationale for refusing the medication.

YOU BE THE JUDGE

THE CASE OF "BEST INTERESTS"

THE FACTS

Roberta Smythe, twenty-seven, a resident of Ontario, was an average undergraduate student. She received her degree in engineering, standing about midway in her class. She applied for a graduate program in engineering and was rejected. She believes that she is a genius and that she stands at the frontier of a new kind of engineering. She has no publications and no reputation, as such, within the academic or professional community.

Smythe also believes that she has been rejected for graduate study (by all five universities to which she applied) because the faculties are envious of her talent and her "vision." On more than one occasion, she has written or emailed individual engineering faculty members threatening their lives unless they "do the right thing." In all other respects, she appears to be a person of normal intelligence.

Because of these threats, Smythe has been arrested and charged. The judge, however, orders that she be given over to a psychiatric facility on the ground that she was not criminally responsible for the threats that she made.

Psychiatrists at the facility where she was placed agree that she suffers from a bipolar disorder (as described in the Starson case). The treatment they propose is the same as was recommended for Starson. Smythe vigorously objects. Her reason: "There is nothing wrong with me. The treatments would destroy my dream and my vision."

The psychiatrists and the Consent and Capacity Board all agree — and there is no evidence to the contrary — that the treatments really would be in her best interests. It is on the basis of Smythe's "best interests" that the CCB find she is not capable of determining consent to the proposed treatments.

THE ISSUE

Are the "best interests" of the patient a basis for determining whether a patient has the capacity to consent to psychiatric treatments?

POINTS TO CONSIDER

- Like Starson, Smythe has not injured anyone. Still, her threats seem real.
- Unlike Starson, Smythe has achieved no recognition in the academic community. But, in her view, this is because, there is a "conspiracy" against her. She sees herself as a great scientist.
- It is a matter of "principle" that causes Smythe to resist the medications proposed by the psychiatrists. She really does not know what the effects of the medications might be.
- Her attending psychiatrists acknowledge that Smythe is intelligent and that they have explained — and she appears to understand — the proposed treatments.
- "On balance," the psychiatrists believe the

treatments will help Smythe out of her "delusions" and make her less threatening.

- The recommendation of the psychiatrists and
  the CCB is based solely but unanimously on
  what they believe to be the "best interests" of
  Smythe. In this regard, they are supported by
  Smythe's mother, father, and siblings, with
  whom she has had a close relationship.

DISCUSSION

The "best interests" of Smythe are not a relevant consideration. The law — that is, the HCCA — determines that it
is not the right of the CCB to determine that she lacks the
capacity to decide upon her own medical treatment, with
the result that drugs could be forced upon her. It does not
matter that there is unanimity for such forced medication
on the part of Smythe's psychiatrists, her family, and the
Board. The Supreme Court of Canada made this clear in
the Starson case.

The Consent and Capacity Board, said Justice Major
for the Court's majority in *Starson*, improperly focused on
what it believed to be in the "best interests" of Starson. And
that was not its duty under the law. Rather, the law required
the Board to ask only this question: Did Starson have the
capacity to decide upon his medical treatment? One's *best*
interests are not, as such, related to capacity to decide.

For the Court majority, Justice Major wrote:

> In my view, the Board's reasons ... appear
> to be overly influenced by its conviction

that medication was in Professor Starson's best interests. The Board arrived at its conclusion by failing to focus on the overriding consideration in this appeal, that is, whether that adult patient had the mental capacity to choose whether to accept or reject the medication prescribed. The enforced injection of mind-altering drugs against [Starson's] will is highly offensive to his dignity and autonomy, and is to be avoided unless it is demonstrated that he lacked the capacity to make his own decision....

As a result of its focus on [Starson's] best interests, the Board disregarded clear evidence of his capacity. Professor Starson acknowledged that he suffered from a mental condition, and appreciated the purpose of the proposed medication and the possible benefits suggested by the doctors. He had tried other treatments in the past to no avail. The evidence did not suggest that enforced treatment was likely to improve his condition.

Professor Starson preferred his altered state to what he viewed as the boredom of normalcy. His primary reason for refusing medication was its dulling effect on his thinking, which prevented his work as a physicist. Although the Board found that he failed to appreciate the possibility that his condition could worsen, [Starson] was never asked about this. Given that he acknowledged the negative impacts of his illness and the need for treatment, it was unreasonable to conclude without further inquiry that he was unable to appreciate that possibility.

THE DISSENT IN *STARSON*

Three members of the Supreme Court, including the chief justice, as noted, dissented in the Starson case. However, the chief justice, who wrote the dissent, suggested that her differences with the majority were not based on any "best interests" test. She said that the Consent and Capacity Board acted on one consideration only: a finding that Starson lacked the capacity required by the HCCA to come to judgment as to his medical needs. She stated:

Nothing in the Board's reasons suggests that it strayed from the question before it — Professor Starson's capacity to make medical decisions on his own behalf. The Board addressed the inquiry at the outset as one involving the criteria "required for an individual to be capable with respect to treatment" and then proceeded to inquire into "capacity." The key to capacity in this case, as discussed, was Professor Starson's ability to appreciate the disorder, its consequences, and possible treatments....

It is ... clear that the Board was concerned with capacity throughout and that its conclusion was driven by evidence relevant to capacity and that alone. Not once does the Board refer to the best interests of the patient.

As a preliminary matter, before entering into its analysis, the Board stated that it viewed Professor Starson's current situation with "great sadness" and stated that "unfortunately, his potential has been disrupted time and time again by admission to psychiatric facilities." But the Board expressly recognized that this was preliminary to analysis as to capacity, not part of that analysis. It began this brief passage with the words: "Before commenting with respect to the specific criteria required for an individual to be capable...." With the greatest of deference, this preliminary comment cannot be elevated to the error of deciding the case on the basis of best interests instead of capacity.

CHALLENGE QUESTION

THE "STANDARD FOR REVIEW"

Was the reviewing court bound to accept the Consent and Capacity Board's conclusion as to Starson's capacity to appreciate the consequences of his decision so long as there was a reasonable basis for doing so?

The Consent and Capacity Board made a number of findings that brought it to the conclusion that, within the meaning of the HCCA, Starson did not have the capacity to decide on his medical treatment. As noted, those findings were reversed by the Ontario Superior Court, whose judgment was affirmed both by the Ontario Court of Appeal and the Supreme Court of Canada. All three courts agreed that findings of fact relating to Starson made by the Board were to be accepted by the courts on review — so long as they had a reasonable basis.

One of the findings that led the board to the conclusion that Starson lacked the necessary capacity was that, under the HCCA, he was not able to appreciate the reasonably foreseeable consequences of his decision not to take the treatments.

Justice Major, for the Court majority, said the issue was one of *law,* not *fact.* The question went to the meaning of that provision of the HCCA: able to appreciate the reasonably foreseeable consequences of a decision. It was for the court alone to determine that meaning. On matters of law, consent boards must yield to the courts.

For the courts to do otherwise, said Justice Major, could well result in different interpretations by different consent boards. There ought to be consistency in application.

How, then, should the provision have been interpreted? Justice Major said the question the board should have asked was why Starson lacked the ability to decide. Justice Major stated:

> The interpretation of the legal standard for capacity is a question of law.... No deference [acceptance, as such] is owed to the

Board on this issue. [T]he broad statutory right of appeal and adjudicative nature of the proceedings militate against deference. Furthermore, courts clearly have relative expertise on general questions of statutory interpretation.

One of the stated purposes of the Act is to provide for the consistent application of its rules. Consistency requires courts to ensure that individual panels do not diverge in their interpretation of statutory provisions. Finally, this question of law has broad application and need not be resolved anew on each appeal. A correctness standard of review on this issue will not impede the expeditious [prompt] treatment of patients.

The Board found that Professor Starson failed to appreciate the risks and benefits of treatment, but neglected to address whether the reasons for that failure demonstrated an inability to appreciate those risks and benefits.

A patient's failure to recognize consequences does not necessarily reflect an inability to appreciate consequences. It is critical that the Board determine whether the reasons for a patient's failure to appreciate consequences demonstrate that the patient is unable, as result of his condition, to appreciate those consequences. In this case, the Board stated that the patient failed

> to appreciate the consequences of treatment
> with regard to future dispositions....
> However, neither of the psychiatrists
> who testified had discussed any of these
> possible consequences with the patient.
> Professor Starson's perceived failure in
> this regard might have simply reflected the
> psychiatrists' failure to inform him of the
> potential consequences.

THE U.S.A. — A DIFFERENT APPROACH?

In a context different from that of Canada, but with Constitutional guarantees similar to those of the Charter of Rights and Freedoms, the U.S. Supreme Court dealt with the question as to whether a mentally ill defendant can be forcibly medicated in order to stand trial. In a 6–3 decision, the Court ruled that, subject to strict restraints, this could be done. The case was that of *Charles Thomas Sell v. United States,* decided June 16, 2003.

There are some obvious similarities with those facts relating to Starson. Sell, a dentist who was well-educated, suffered from delusions. Though he had threatened others, including FBI agents, he had a non-violent history (as did Starson) — at least as was found by the trial court.

In 1997 Sell was charged with submitting false insurance claims to the U.S. federal government (Medicaid). The court found that he was not competent to stand trial. In 1999 the court committed him to a mental institution for treatment that, if possible, would permit trial.

His attending psychiatrists proposed mood-affecting medications (anti-psychotic drugs) but, as with Starson, Sell strongly objected. His reasons were different from those of Starson. Sell believed that a conspiracy had been mounted against him by the federal government, including the FBI. Starson, it will be recalled, believed that anti-psychotic drugs, which had been tried on him earlier, had dulled his brain and, if given to him again (even though they were of a different kind), would deny him the capacity to function as a scientist.

The issue in *Starson* was whether, having been found not criminally responsible (NCR) for threatening the lives of several persons and then placed in a mental institution, he could, as part of his treatment, be forcibly medicated. The issue in Sell was whether the defendant, mentally ill, could be forcibly medicated for the purpose of standing trial for the charges made against him.

THE U.S. CONSTITUTION APPLIED

Applied to both federal and state action in the United States, one's liberty is protected by the due process provisions of the U.S. Constitution. In Canada, life, liberty, and the security of the person are guaranteed by section 7 of the Charter of Rights and Freedoms, part of the Constitution of Canada.

This is how Justice Stephen Breyer, speaking for the U.S. Supreme Court majority in *Sell*, summarized the balance struck by the Court in reconciling the rights of the individual with the need to protect the public and allow for a fair trial (which is included within the protective circle of due process). He stated:

> [The U.S.] Constitution permits the Government involuntarily to administer anti-psychotic drugs to a mentally ill defendant facing serious criminal charges in order to render that defendant competent to stand trial, but only if the treatment is medically appropriate, is substantially unlikely to have side effects that may undermine the fairness

of the trial, and, taking account of less intrusive alternatives, is necessary significantly to further important governmental trial-related interests.

The standards required by the Court before medications can be forced on a defendant are difficult for the government to meet. Justice Breyer said that the instances when the government will meet such standards likely will be "rare." He wrote of the standards:

> First, a court must find that important governmental interests are at stake. The Government's interest in bringing to trial an individual accused of a serious crime is important. That is so whether the offense is a serious crime against the person or a serious crime against property. In both instances, the Government seeks to protect through application of the criminal law the basic human need for security....
>
> Second, the court must conclude that involuntary medication will significantly further those ... state interests. It must find that administration of the drugs is substantially likely to render the defendant competent to stand trial. At the same time, it must find that administration of the drugs is substantially unlikely to have side effects that will interfere significantly with the defendant's ability to assist counsel in conducting a trial defense, thereby rendering the trial unfair.
>
> Third, the court must conclude that involuntary medication is necessary to further those interests. The court must find that any alternative, less intrusive treatments are unlikely to achieve substantially the same results [such as non-drug therapies, like — as with Starson — psychotherapy],

and the possible use of court orders backed by its contempt power to order certain action on the part of the defendant....

Fourth, as we have said, the court must conclude that administration of the drugs is medically appropriate, i.e., in the patient's best medical interest in light of his medical condition. The specific kinds of drugs at issue may matter here as elsewhere. Different kinds of anti-psychotic drugs may produce different side effects and enjoy different levels of success.

We emphasize that the court applying these standards is seeking to determine whether involuntary administration of drugs is necessary significantly to further a particular governmental interest, namely, the interest in rendering the defendant competent to stand trial.

THE FUTURE FOR DR. SELL?

The U.S. Supreme Court ruled that the government had not justified forcing anti-psychotic medications on Sell. However, the ruling does not prohibit the U.S. government from attempting to meet the standards required by the Court for forcing such medications.

What is the likelihood that the government will satisfy the standards imposed by the U.S. Supreme Court? The government probably will not be able to satisfy at least one important test: The government may not be able to prove that it has a real interest in bringing Sell to trial. The reason: A defendant ordinarily receives credit toward a sentence for time already served. In the case of Sell, he was confined by the mental institution for more than four years — a time well beyond that to which he would have been sentenced.

Justice Breyer expanded on the connection between the government's interest and that of the individual as to the standards ordered:

> Courts, however, must consider the facts of the individual case in evaluating the Government's interest in prosecution. Special circumstances may lessen the importance of that interest. The defendant's failure to take drugs voluntarily, for example, may mean lengthy confinement in an institution for the mentally ill — and that would diminish the risks that ordinarily attach to freeing without punishment one who has committed a serious crime.
>
> We do not mean to suggest that civil commitment is a substitute for a criminal trial. The Government has a substantial interest in timely prosecution. And it may be difficult or impossible to try a defendant who regains competence after years of commitment during which memories may fade and evidence may be lost. The potential for future confinement affects, but does not totally undermine, the strength of the need for prosecution. The same is true of the possibility that the defendant has already been confined for a significant amount of time (for which he would receive credit toward any sentence ultimately imposed). Moreover, the Government has a [corresponding] constitutionally essential interest in assuring that the defendant's trial is a fair one.

CIVIL REMEDY: ANOTHER APPROACH

The Starson case involved government action to have an individual, then held in a mental institution as not criminally responsible

(NCR) for alleged violations of the Criminal Code, forced to take anti-psychotic drugs, ostensibly to help control a bipolar disorder. Unlike the Sell case in the United States, the action proposed for Starson was not to help make him competent to stand trial.

The court in *Starson* was not asked — and thus it did not offer — any opinion as to whether Starson was in the kind of condition that would permit, on proper application, the appointment of a guardian to act on his behalf. Such an appointment would come outside the Criminal Code. Yet, even here, the basic finding that Starson did not wish to have the drugs proposed would have had the effect — to the extent that desire was expressed at a point when Starson was fully competent.

YOU BE THE JUDGE

THE CASE OF FORCED CONFINEMENT

The case that follows was decided by the Supreme Court of Canada on the same day as *Starson*. You will see that it does not involve forced medication. It does, however, relate to action by the Crown to forcibly control over a period of years an individual found to be, as was Starson, not criminally responsible.

THE FACTS

Terry Steven Owen had a long history of conflict with the criminal law. Before 1978, his record included offences for breaking and entering, obstructing a police officer, trafficking in narcotics, possession of narcotics, and possession of stolen property. But it was in 1978 that Owen was brought into contact with another custodial force of society: the mental health system. It was a contact that continued to apply at least through 2003.

On October 10, 1978, Owen was found not guilty, by reason of a mental disorder, of a charge of second degree murder. It was determined that he had been in a psychotic state induced by drug abuse. Owen was found not criminally responsible (NCR) for the murder.

The circumstances of the murder (called the "index offence") were as follows. Owen had been living with a young man from Chatham, Ontario, for about three months. He only remembered being "paranoid" for "some weeks prior to the offence and that he had this song in his head."

The night before the murder, Owen ate an apple spiked with MDA, a hallucinogenic drug. He said he became frightened. He believed that his friend had helped to murder his grandfather (who, in fact, had died from natural causes sometime earlier). He began to hit his friend with a stick. Police arrived and Owen was arrested and charged with murder.

For Owen, there followed periods of detention in various mental health care institutions. However, he was gradually released into the community until 1987, when he was arrested on charges of possession of a prohibited weapon, break and enter with intent to commit an indictable offence, and possession of property obtained by crime. On June 15, 1988, he was convicted of all three charges.

After completing his sentence, Owen was returned to a psychiatric hospital. In 1989 he got into a disagreement with the staff about hospital privileges. He lost his self-control and punched a car door so hard that he broke bones in his hand, requiring a cast. He was reported to have said: "It was either the door or Brad's jaw. Man, I had to hit something."

In 1990, while living in the community, Owen fractured a man's jaw with a pool cue during an argument while under the influence of alcohol. He was convicted of assault causing bodily harm and was sentenced to fourteen months in prison, which he served before returning to the psychiatric hospital.

The facility continued to gradually release Owen into the general community, but the problems with substance abuse as well as violent outbursts did not end.

A 1992 risk assessment conducted by the Ontario Ministry of Health placed Owen in a category of violent offenders for which it was predicted that 44 percent would re-offend violently within seven years after release. The psychiatric hospital said of him:

> [Owen's] prognosis continued to be extremely guarded given his lack of insight into his situation, his lack of regard for other persons, and his intolerance of the system. It was predicted that a circumstantial situation will likely compromise his liberty at an early stage in community living. [Owen] has a history of repeated offences, including unprovoked violence, indulgence in drugs and alcohol, and a cavalier attitude, making him a serious risk to the community.

Still, from 1994 to 1996, Owen received from the Ontario Review Board (which had the statutory power) "conditional discharges," subject to ongoing drug tests from the psychiatric hospital. The tests were designed to ensure that he did not use drugs.

In 1997, however, Owen's urine tested positive for cannabis. The hospital informed the Board that it could no longer support Owen's conditional discharge because of his continued substance abuse and the hospital's need for flexibility "to react quickly to known increases in risk." The hospital stated:

> When the hospital is unable to require either hospital admission or significant changes in supervision [as a result of Owen's conditional discharge], the community is placed at risk. The community would fail to appreciate why it is that [the hospital] is unable to react quickly to known increases in risk. This situation is very likely to occur time and time again in the future. The role of the hospital should be to ensure that it is managed in a timely manner, consistent with the long-term rehabilitation needs of [Owen] and not contrary to the safety of the public. The hospital sees no useful purpose in a several month hospitalization every time this happens while [Owen] awaits the pleasure of the Board. Indeed the results of the current administrative arrangement [a conditional release] are contrary to the rehabilitation

needs of [Owen] and do nothing to protect
the public....

Nevertheless, for three years, from 1997 to 1999, the
Ontario Review Board allowed Owen to live in Kingston,
Ontario, but to be "detained" by the psychiatric hospital.
As in the past, the conditions were that he continue to be
tested and abstain from drugs. (The testing was to be done
at the psychiatric hospital.)

In 1999 the hospital "team" reported: "[Owen] continues to represent a risk to the safety of the public." The
next year, the hospital, on closely monitored tests, detected
Owen's continued use of cocaine. The hospital was told —
and Owen later admitted — that he had "faked" a number
of drug tests, and that he had been using drugs, except for
an eighteen-month period before the birth of his son (to
whom the Court stated he was "devoted"). Indeed, Owen
indicated that he had no intention of abandoning his use
of drugs.

The Board, following a full hearing, found that Owen
continued to be a significant danger to the safety of the
public. It ordered his continued detention at the psychiatric
hospital (a medium security facility). This meant, among
other things, that Owen could not live in the community.
Nor could he visit in the community without attendants
from the hospital.

THE ISSUE

Does Owen, having been found not criminally responsible
for a murder in 1978, have an absolute right to discharge

from the psychiatric hospital? In effect, did Owen have the right to go free in 2003?

POINTS TO CONSIDER

- Under the Criminal Code (sections 16(1) and 672.34), a person found not criminally responsible (NCR) for what has been charged is not acquitted. Rather, that person is judged not to have known the "nature or quality" of the act resulting in the crime.
- There is no presumption that an NCR individual is a danger to the safety of the public.
- If, however, a court or review board finds that an NCR individual does pose a significant risk to public safety, then it might enter an order restraining that person.
- Under section 672.54 of the Criminal Code, the order, called a disposition, must be the "least onerous and least restrictive to the accused" consistent with the level of risk posed. Such an order can range from detention "in a hospital" to discharge "subject to such conditions as the court or review board considers appropriate."
- It is central to the constitutionality of the NCR provisions that the individual not be considered punished, but rather that the conditions imposed on him are for the protection of the public. Owen has argued that he is being punished for his drug habit and his failure to

cooperate with hospital authorities from 1978 to 2000 (e.g., drug testing).

- The decision of the Ontario Review Board is subject to appeal to the courts. But, the courts must accept the Board's decision so long as it appears to be reasonable, and the hearings before the Board were conducted fairly. In the case of Owen, the Ontario Court of Appeal overturned the judgment of the Board on the ground that it was unreasonable: He was being held because of his drug habit, not because of his mental condition. And, he was not a significant risk to the public.

- At least once each year, the Board must examine and decide upon its existing order. In addition, it may — on the request, for example, of Owen — review its order at any time. The Board must be satisfied that there is reasonable evidence for continuing to detain the NCR individual. Otherwise, it must unconditionally release him/her.

- There is no fixed term for confinement of an NCR person. He/she might be held in the mental institution far longer (even for life) than the Criminal Code would impose for punishment.

DISCUSSION

The case *The Queen v. Terry Steven Owen* was decided June 6, 2003. In an 8–1 decision, with Justice Ian Binnie speaking for the majority and Justice Louise Arbour dissenting, the

Supreme Court of Canada ruled that the Ontario Review Board decision should be upheld and the Ontario Court of Appeal judgment reversed.

In large part, Justice Binnie said, the Board had been set up by statute to give expert opinion. So long as that opinion, based on the facts, was reasonable, and a fair hearing had been granted, then there was no basis for the Ontario Court of Appeal to reverse the Board decision.

The facts, said Justice Binnie, justified the Board's actions: Owen had murdered in 1978 because of the use of drugs. They caused him to lose control. He was found by the trial court to not be criminally responsible for the death of his friend. The underlying cause of Owen's actions — the use of drugs and alcohol — did not end in 1978. Rather, they continued, unknown to the medical staff of the psychiatric hospital. They continued because Owen faked the tests the hospital had imposed as part of the terms of his conditional releases ordered by the Ontario Review Board. And, during that period, on a number of occasions, Owen was involved in acts or threats of violence against others. Indeed, in one instance he served a prison sentence of fourteen months for such an assault.

From the viewpoint of the hospital staff, communicated to the Board, Owen remained a significant danger to the community (as well as to himself). There was no way to control his drug habit — which set in motion his irrational behaviour — other than by direct control, and this meant his continued detention. This was the least onerous way — at the present time — to protect the public.

THE STANDARD OF REASONABLENESS APPLIED

Justice Binnie, for the Court, stated:

Having thus affirmed as reasonable the Board's conclusion that [Owen] continues to be a significant threat to the safety of the public, I turn to the issue ... [of] whether the Board's ... order is the least onerous and least restrictive for [Owen] consistent with the assurance of public safety. In considering its order, the Board must again have regard to the need to protect the public from dangerous persons, the mental condition of the [NCR] accused, the reintegration of the [NCR] accused into society, and the other needs of the [NCR] accused.

As mentioned, from 1994 to 1996, [Owen] was granted conditional discharge orders. This was changed in 1997 because of drug use. A detention order with leave conditions was substituted. That detention order was continued in 1998 and 1999. In 2000, the "leave conditions" were made more restrictive because of the discovery, on January 25, 2000, that [Owen] was on cocaine. At that point, in making its recommendation, the hospital staff told the Board that: "In the presence of close supervision, [Owen] consumed illicit substances. *In the absence of direct supervision at all times*, the hospital is not confident in its ability to prevent [Owen] from engaging in these risky behaviours [emphasis added]."

Accordingly, in [the hospital's] view, given the link it had made between [Owen's] propensity for violence and the use of cocaine, the hospital detention order with restricted leave conditions represented "the least onerous and restrictive, in keeping with the need to protect the safety of the public."

The success or failure of an NCR detainee to follow a treatment program was noted as a relevant factor [for the Board to consider].

The Board was clearly sympathetic to [Owen's] desire to be reunited with his son and his evident level of frustration at his continued detention. The critical factor that tilted the Board against a less restrictive order was [Owen's] renewed (or rediscovered) taking of cocaine, and its pharmacological link to the amphetamines that triggered the 1978 murder. This discovery led the hospital authorities to recommend against a conditional release....

DIRECT CONTROL: THE LEAST RESTRICTIVE
Justice Binnie continued:

The Board agreed with the hospital that there was little prospect of [Owen's] drug habit being effectively controlled with the sort of sporadic supervision available in the community. The Board recognized the ease with which [Owen] had deceived its drug monitoring program in the past. In light of the connection between [Owen's] violence and the newly discovered cocaine abuse, the Board concluded:

"It is unfortunate that [Owen] has chosen to retard his progress toward rehabilitation and thwart the efforts of his caregivers to return him to society. We note that as recently as August of 1999, the treatment team were prepared to support his transfer to the Chatham area, which remains [Owen's] desired relocation. [Owen] by his conduct is the agent of his own misfortune, albeit he is unlikely to recognize or appreciate his role in what he will undoubtedly determine to be punishment by the Review Board and the hospital."

I do not think it unreasonable for the Board to conclude, in light of the difficulty in monitoring the cocaine problem in the community, that the "least onerous and least restrictive" order for the time being was a detention order in [the psychiatric hospital].

[Owen's] case is not an easy one, but once we affirm as reasonable the Board's finding that [Owen] represents a "significant threat to the safety of the public," we should not be too quick to overturn the Board's expert opinion about how that risk is to be managed....

HOPE FOR OWEN?

Owen's case came before the Supreme Court of Canada three years after the Ontario Review Board's last detention order was issued. And, the fact is that as an NCR, as noted, he could be subject to ongoing detention for the rest of his life — so long as he continued his drug habit, and so long as the Board believed that that drug habit was connected with his violent behaviour.

Justice Binnie seemed to hold out hope for Owen (and other NCRs). That hope came in the form of guaranteed annual review by the Board. It is a review in which the Crown must prove that the NCR continues to be a significant threat to the community and that the least restrictive way to contain that threat, bearing in mind as well the interests of the individual, is through ongoing detention.

Owen, however, offered the Court another solution. He proposed that if he continued to use prohibited drugs, then why not let the criminal process treat him "like anyone else"? Lay charges and, if he is found guilty, impose an appropriate sentence.

The answer given by Justice Binnie, for the Court, is that an NCR is not like anyone else. He or she is subject to special treatment under Part XX.1 of the Criminal Code.

THE DISSENT OF JUSTICE ARBOUR

Justice Arbour did not question Owen's use of drugs. Nor did she question his violent actions. What she did question, among other things, was whether in the first instance — in the period following the 1978 murder — he continued to be subject to mental illness. His illness, at least as described by the psychiatric hospital, was anti-social behaviour. She stated:

> [Owen] has been and may continue to be in con-
> flict with the law. He has been and most likely
> would continue to be answerable to the criminal
> justice system for such behaviour. He has com-
> mitted a most serious offence for which he was
> held not criminally responsible as a result of his
> mental condition at the time.
>
> The question now is whether his mental con-
> dition and the threat he may pose to the public
> are such as to require his continued handling
> by the special stream created by Part XX.1 of
> the Criminal Code, which places emphasis on
> "achieving the twin goals of protecting the pub-
> lic and treating the mentally ill offender fairly and
> appropriately."

The Board did find that Mr. Owen suffers from a "serious antisocial personality disorder".... While each of these personality attributes is clearly undesirable, the syndrome is not itself a mental illness but rather an assortment of symptoms which reflect poor adjustment to society.... In my view, both the hospital officials and the members of the Board were unduly influenced by the recent discovery that Mr. Owen had regularly cheated on his drug and alcohol tests in the past. It had always been known that [he] was likely to be engaging in substance abuse. To restrict [Owen's] freedom severely after finding that he had deceived the hospital indicates that at its root the disposition was punitive in purpose. I agree with the Court of Appeal that the Board's assessment of the risk posed by [Owen] was entirely speculative and not supported by a proper appreciation of the record.

The present case raises the issue of the extent and limits of the "special stream" designed for mentally ill people. It is not a special stream that permits the perpetual detention of regular delinquents who have once committed a crime while suffering from a mental disorder. The commission of an "index offence" [the 1978 murder by Owen] does place an individual within the NCR system, but there is no indication in the statutory scheme that the differential treatment of NCR accused and members of the general population is meant to be indefinite — in fact, the opposite is clearly the case. [A past Court decision] establishes that the threshold determination for taking an individual out of the NCR system is the determination of significant threat to the community. That threat has to be assessed in light of several factors, including the mental condition of the accused....

[Owen] had been in the NCR system for 22 years and had been the subject of 24 disposition or warrant orders when the Board rendered the decision under appeal. He did live in the community under different forms of supervision for extended periods of time commencing in 1986, and he resided full-time in the community from 1994 until this disposition was taken.

Under this March 2000 disposition, [Owen] was ordered detained in hospital without entry into the community except under escort. This was the most restrictive disposition imposed upon him since 1990, after his conviction for assault, and, apart from that one, the most restrictive since 1982. The Board ordered detention in hospital with only compassionate leave and staff-accompanied entry into the community. It gave no reason for its conclusion that this most restrictive disposition was "the least onerous and least restrictive" one. In my view this disposition constituted an error of law and was not reasonable.

Even on the assumption that [Owen] constituted a sufficient threat to the community to preclude his absolute discharge, the Board was required to embark on an evaluation of all four of the factors outlined in §672.54 — the need to protect the public from dangerous persons, the mental condition of the accused, the reintegration of the accused into society and the other needs of the accused — in order to determine whether a conditional discharge or a custodial order was the appropriate disposition.

This could not adequately be done without considering that [Owen] had lived in the community since 1994, that no violent incident occurred in a period of close to 10 years, [Owen's] desire to be reunited with his son, and the fact that despite his failure to abstain from substance abuse he had nonetheless made some successful efforts in recent years to manage various stressors in his life. In my view, on the facts of this case, it was unreasonable for the Board to conclude that the custodial disposition imposed was the least onerous disposition available in the circumstances in that it accorded the respondent "as much liberty as is compatible with public safety."

REFERENCES AND FURTHER READING

* Cited by the Supreme Court of Canada.

Bailey, Sue. "Physics Genius Cannot Be Forcibly Medicated for Mental Illness: SCOC." *Canadian Press,* June 6, 2003.

Berg, Jessica et al. *Informed Consent: Legal Theory and Clinical Practice,* 2nd ed. Oxford University Press, 2001.*

Greenhouse, Linda. "[U.S.] Supreme Court Limits Forced Medication of Some for Trial." *New York Times,* June 17, 2003.

Hoffman, Brian F. *The Law of Consent to Treatment in Ontario,* 2nd ed. Butterworths, Toronto, 1997.*

Macklin, Ruth. "Some Problems in Gaining Informed Consent from Psychiatric Patients." *Emory Law Journal* 345 (1982): 31.*

Makin, Kirk. "High Court Supports Mentally-ill Physicist." *Globe and Mail,* June 7, 2003.

"Mentally Ill 'Genius' Can Refuse Drugs, Court Says." *Toronto Star*, June 6, 2003.

Roth, Loren H., Alan Meisel, and Charles W. Lidz. "Tests of Competency to Consent to Treatment." *American Journal of Psychiatry* 279 (1997): 134.*

Tyler, Tracey. "Bright Mind, No Bright Future." *Toronto Star*, June 7, 2003.

Weisstub, David N. *Enquiry on Mental Competency: Final Report.* Toronto: Queen's Printer for Ontario 1990.*

Wente, Margaret. "The Case of the Crazy Professor." *Globe and Mail*, June 10, 2003.

CHAPTER 3

MERCY KILLING: A DEFENCE TO MURDER?

Can "mercy" killing ever be a defence to a charge of murder? In a strictly legal sense, the answer must be no. However, there is a process that may bend the outcome: a trial before a jury that alone has the power to find on the facts that the accused is guilty or innocent, and a judge who alone has the power to sentence and, in doing so, may exercise a measure of discretion.

Among the questions raised in this chapter are:

- May the defence bring to a jury the facts that "forced" the accused to mercy killing?
- To what extent, if any, may a jury consider those facts in coming to its verdict?
- May those facts be used by a judge to "temper" a sentence?

These questions were explored in a case decided by the Supreme Court of Canada on June 14, 2001 (*Latimer v. The Queen* [2001] 1 *Supreme Court of Canada Reports* 3).

Robert Latimer, a Saskatchewan farmer, intentionally ended the life of his twelve-year-old daughter, Tracy, who had suffered from a severe form of cerebral palsy since birth. To many, Latimer's action was mercy killing by a concerned and conflicted parent. To others, his action was murder.

The Crown prosecuted Latimer on the charge of murder in the first degree. A jury found him guilty of the lesser offence of murder in the second degree. The Criminal Code required (a) that Latimer be given a life sentence with a minimum term in prison of ten years, and (b) that he not be eligible for parole (release) during that time.

In fact, Latimer was tried twice and he was found guilty of second degree murder each time. The first conviction brought a life sentence with a minimum term of ten years in prison without the opportunity for parole. However, this conviction was thrown out because the Crown had interfered with the jury selection process.

On appeal, the Supreme Court of Canada ordered a new trial. It is that new trial and the resulting sentence on conviction that will be set out here.

These are among the issues explored in the case:

- Did Latimer have the right to present to the jury a defence of "necessity" when the judge believed that there was no real basis for the claim?
- Did the jury have a right to recommend what it believed to be a fair sentence even though the Criminal Code, as enacted by Parliament, set the minimum required sentence (ten years)?
- Based on the facts, is the required minimum sentence of life in prison for ten years without the possibility of parole "cruel and unusual punishment" within the meaning of the Canadian Charter of Rights and Freedoms and thus open for modification? That is, does a trial judge have the right to change a sentence otherwise required by statute in order to make it comply with the Charter?
- May a jury, in effect, "nullify" what would otherwise be

a conviction required by law? May a jury consciously put the law to the side and do what it believes to be just?

- Is it possible for a sentence to be set aside once it has been lawfully imposed by a court?

We will begin with a detailed description of the facts of the case. We will set out the extent of Tracy Latimer's illness, how she responded to treatment, and how her father cared for but finally killed his daughter. Then, we will move to the issues raised before the Supreme Court of Canada, and how the Court responded to them.

TRACY LATIMER'S ILLNESS, TREATMENT, AND DEATH

The description of Tracy Latimer's illness, treatment, and death that follows was given by the Court. Tracy, as noted, had suffered from a severe form of cerebral palsy since birth. She was quadriplegic and, as such, was unable to use either her arms or her legs. She was bedridden for much of the time. Her condition was permanent, caused by neurological damage. She had the mental capacity of a four-month-old baby, though she could — and did — communicate with others through facial expressions, laughter, and crying.

The Court stated: "Tracy enjoyed music, bonfires, being with her family, and the circus. She liked to play music on a radio, which she could use with a special button. Tracy could apparently recognize family members and she would express joy at seeing them. Tracy also loved being rocked gently by her parents."

Tracy was completely dependent on others for her care, in which family members, including her father, were involved. She had frequent seizures — five to six each day (in the nature of epilepsy). And, said the Court, it was thought that she experienced a great deal of pain, which could not be relieved by medication because that would conflict with her anti-epileptic medication. She had to be spoon-fed, and her lack of nutrients caused weight loss.

There was evidence that Tracy could have been fed with a feeding tube inserted into her stomach, an option that would have improved her nutrition and health, and might also have allowed for pain medication to be administered. But the Latimers rejected the feeding tube option as being intrusive. They saw it as representing the first step on a path to preserving Tracy's life "artificially."

TREATMENT: SURGERIES AND PAIN

There was no doubt in the Court's view that Tracy had a serious disability, but she was not terminally ill. Her life was not in its final stages. In the view of her doctors, there were other treatments, including surgical procedures, required in part to ease her difficulty breathing.

Tracy had already undergone several surgeries in her short lifetime. In 1990, surgery was used to balance the muscles around her pelvis. In 1992, it was used to reduce the abnormal curvature in her back.

The Court stated: "Like the majority of totally involved, quadriparetic children with cerebral palsy, Tracy had developed scoliosis, an abnormal curvature and rotation in the back, necessitating surgery to implant metal rods to support her spine. While it was a successful procedure, further problems developed in Tracy's right hip: It became dislocated and caused her considerable pain."

Tracy was scheduled to undergo further surgery on November 19, 1993. This was to deal with her dislocated hip and, it was hoped, to lessen her constant pain. The procedure involved removing her upper thigh bone, which would leave her lower leg loose without any connecting bone. (Her leg would be held in place only by muscle and tissue). The anticipated recovery period for this surgery was one year.

The Latimers were told that this procedure would cause pain, and the doctors involved said that further surgery would be required to relieve the pain coming from various joints in Tracy's body. This surgery was seen by the Latimers as "mutilation." Robert Latimer concluded that his daughter's life was not "worth living."

TRACY'S DEATH

In the weeks leading up to Tracy's death in October 1993, the Latimers looked into the possibility of placing her in a group home in nearby North Battleford. She had lived there between July and October of that year while her mother was pregnant. The Latimers went so far as to apply to place Tracy in the home. Later, however, they changed their minds.

On October 12, 1993, after learning that Tracy's doctors wished to perform the additional surgery, Robert Latimer decided to end his daughter's life. On Sunday, October 24, 1993, while his wife and Tracy's siblings were at church, Robert Latimer carried Tracy to his pickup truck, seated her in the cab, inserted a hose from the truck's exhaust pipe into the cab, and turned on the engine. She died from the carbon monoxide.

The police conducted an autopsy and discovered carbon monoxide in her blood. Robert Latimer at first maintained that Tracy simply passed away in her sleep. He later confessed to having taken her life, gave a statement to the investigating police, and partially re-enacted his actions on videotape. Latimer also told police that he had considered giving Tracy an overdose of Valium, or "shooting her in the head."

The Crown charged Latimer with first degree murder.

ROBERT LATIMER'S SECOND TRIAL

In the face of Latimer's confession and the facts surrounding Tracy's death, these questions were raised by his defence:

- What legal defence could Latimer have to the charge of first degree murder?
- How could a jury return a verdict of "not guilty"?
- On what basis could a jury or a trial judge, on a finding of guilt, impose a lighter sentence than that ordered by statute?

The answers in large part rested in an apparent three-part strategy by the defence:

1. to give a jury a "legal" basis to acquit Latimer;
2. to convince the jury that, regardless of the law, Latimer should be excused on the facts; and
3. if that failed, then, regardless of the minimum term set out by the Criminal Code, Latimer should be given a "light" sentence, not the ten-year imprisonment meted out to violent offenders.

(The defence seemed to be relying on a sympathetic jury composed of people who lived in the same area as Latimer.)

We shall consider each point, and set out the trial court's rulings, as well as those of the appeal court and the Supreme Court of Canada.

RULINGS OF THE TRIAL AND APPELLATE COURT

The "defence" urged by Latimer was that of *necessity*. That is, Tracy, who was in great pain, should not have had to undergo the additional medical treatments. For her, there was no other recourse than to have her life ended by her father.

The defence brought out these facts in the trial. In closing arguments, the defence asked the trial court judge to rule that the jury could consider the defence of necessity. The judge refused to give a ruling at that time. But, at the end of closing arguments, the judge ruled that the defence was not available to Latimer. That is, the judge stated, the law in no way could be read as allowing the defence argued by Latimer and, as such, it could not be considered by the jury.

Next, the jury asked the trial judge if they could have any input into the sentence should they find him guilty. The trial judge replied that the jury's job was to determine the guilt or innocence of Latimer. After this was done, said the judge, there might be room for a jury recommendation as to sentence. The trial judge stated:

> The penalty in any of these charges is not the concern of the jury. Your concern is, as I said, the guilt or innocence of the accused, you must reach — that's your job, you reach that conclusion, and don't concern yourself with what the penalty might be. We say that because we don't want you to be influenced one way or the other with what that penalty is. So it may be that later on, once you have reached a verdict, you — we will have some discussions about that, but not at this stage of the game. You must just carry on and answer the question that was put to you, okay.

What the judge did not tell the jury was that the statute under which Latimer was tried required, on a finding of guilt, a minimum sentence of imprisonment of ten years. If the trial judge had told this to the jury, then there might have been the possibility of nullification. That is, said the defence, the jury might have opted to ignore the law and acquit Latimer.

The jury found Latimer guilty of second degree murder. It was then that the judge told the jury of the required minimum sentence. In law, the only recommendation the jury could make upon which the trial judge could act was whether to increase the minimum sentence (up to a maximum of twenty-five years). However, the judge did permit the jury to suggest a sentence. And, the jury suggested one year imprisonment before the eligibility of parole.

The judge then handed down his sentence. Because, in his view, a ten-year sentence would have violated Latimer's Charter right against cruel and unusual punishment, he ordered a sentence of one year in prison and one year probation with Latimer confined to his farm.

There was an appeal to the Saskatchewan Court of Appeal. That court affirmed the conviction. Then, however, it rejected the trial court's sentence. It ordered instead that Latimer serve the minimum ten-year sentence of imprisonment, without the possibility of parole during that time.

TIMING

Latimer asked the trial judge to rule that the defence of necessity was available after all the evidence had been submitted and just before closing arguments. Defence counsel said that he had two versions for closing arguments: (1) if the defence were allowed, or (2) if the defence were refused.

The trial judge said he would rule on the defence *after* closing arguments had been made. However, it should be noted that the defence, in closing arguments, certainly referred to the evidence which would have gone into the defence of necessity — if it had been allowed.

THE SUPREME COURT OF CANADA DECIDES

The issues raised before the trial court and the court of appeal were presented to the Supreme Court of Canada.

There are nine members on the Court. Ordinarily, the opinion of the Court — whether it is a majority opinion or even a unanimous decision — is announced by one of the justices. His/her name is attached to the opinion. However, in the Latimer case, the opinion was announced as that of "the Court." No individual justice's name was attached to the opinion. The significance: By setting this as the opinion of the Court, its reasoning and conclusions take on a more forceful meaning.

There were three major parts in the Court's opinion:

1. "necessity" as a defence for the jury to consider;
2. the right to the opportunity for jury nullification; and
3. the mandatory sentence as cruel and unusual punishment.

"NECESSITY" AS A DEFENCE FOR THE JURY
TO CONSIDER

Based on the law and the facts, the Court stated, there simply was no basis on which a jury could even consider the possibility of the defence of "necessity." There was, in the words of the Court, "no air of reality" to the claim of "necessity." In this regard, the Court first set out the legal requirements that go to make up the defence of necessity. Then, it looked to the facts involving Latimer.

The defence of necessity is one created by the common law, but it has, at its core, important values that will not hold individuals liable under the criminal law where they acted *involuntarily* and, more particularly, where their actions were taken *under duress*. The Court cited the leading case of *Perka v. The Queen*, [1984]

2 *Supreme Court of Canada Reports* 232, where then Justice Brian Dickson (later chief justice) said:

> [The defence of necessity] rests on a realistic assessment of human weakness, recognizing that a liberal and humane criminal law cannot hold people to the strict obedience of laws in emergency situations where normal human instincts, whether of self-preservation or of altruism, overwhelmingly impel disobedience. The objectivity of the criminal law is preserved; such acts are still wrongful, but in the circumstances they are excusable. Praise is indeed not bestowed, but pardon is....

Justice Dickson insisted that the defence of necessity be limited to those rare cases in which true "involuntariness" is present. The defence, he held, must be "strictly controlled and scrupulously limited."

The decision in *Perka* outlined three elements that must be present for the defence of necessity. The Court gave specific content to these elements:

1. *Imminent peril.* There must, said the Court, be an urgent situation of "clear and imminent peril." Disaster must be imminent, or harm unavoidable and near. It is not enough that the peril is foreseeable or likely; it must be on the verge of happening and virtually certain to occur. Patience, itself, must be seen as "unreasonable." If the accused could reasonably have avoided the situation of peril, there was a duty to do so.

2. *No reasonable legal alternative to disobeying the law.* If there were a reasonable legal alternative to breaking the law, then there is no basis for arguing necessity. The accused need not

be placed in the last resort imaginable, but he/she must have no reasonable legal alternative. If an alternative to breaking the law exists, the defence of necessity fails.

3. *Proportionality.* There must be proportionality between the harm inflicted and the harm avoided. This means that the harm inflicted must not be disproportionate to the harm the accused sought to avoid. Put somewhat differently, the harm avoided must clearly be greater than the harm inflicted. Justice Dickson said in *Perka*: "No rational criminal justice system, no matter how humane or liberal, could excuse the infliction of a greater harm to allow the actor to avert a lesser evil. In such circumstances we expect the individual to bear the harm and refrain from acting illegally. If he cannot control himself, we will not excuse him."

IMMINENT PERIL

On appeal, the Supreme Court of Canada was *not* asked to determine whether the necessity defence had been proved by Latimer. Rather, the Court was only asked to decide whether there had been enough merit in Latimer's claim to the defence for it to be put to the jury. Recall that defence counsel asked the trial judge to rule on whether the necessity defence could be put to the jury — *after all the evidence had been heard and the defence was at the point of closing argument.*

The test that the trial judge used to answer the question was whether there was an air of reality to the claim of necessity. If the trial judge had answered that question *yes,* then a jury, properly instructed, would have had to weigh the evidence and, if it believed Latimer, to enter a verdict of acquittal.

But, as noted, the trial judge simply could find no real basis to the defence; and, the Supreme Court of Canada agreed with this finding. The Supreme Court stated that not one of the three factors necessary for proof of necessity had been put forward by Latimer.

(And, each of those factors would have had to be proved.) The Court stated:

> The first requirement [of] imminent peril ... is not met in this case. [Latimer] does not suggest he himself faced any peril; instead, he identifies a peril to his daughter, stemming from her upcoming surgery which he perceived as a form of mutilation. Acute suffering can constitute imminent peril, but in this case there was nothing in her medical condition that placed Tracy in a dangerous situation where death was an alternative. Tracy was thought to be in pain before the surgery, and that pain was expected to continue, or increase, following the surgery. But that ongoing pain did not constitute an emergency in this case....
>
> Tracy's proposed surgery did not pose an imminent threat to her life, nor did her medical condition. In fact, Tracy's health might have improved had Latimer not rejected the option of relying on a feeding tube. Tracy's situation was not an emergency. [Latimer] can be reasonably expected to have understood that reality.
>
> There was no evidence of a legitimate psychological condition that rendered [Latimer] unable to perceive that there was no imminent peril. [Latimer] argued that, for him, further surgery did amount to imminent peril. It was not reasonable for [Latimer] to form this belief, particularly when better pain management was available.

The Court went on to examine each of the other factors required to prove "necessity" even though it would have been enough to have ended with its discussion of imminent peril.

NO REASONABLE LEGAL ALTERNATIVE TO DISOBEYING THE LAW

With regard to *no reasonable legal alternative,* the Court stated:

> In this case, there is no air of reality to the proposition that [Latimer] had no reasonable legal alternative to killing his daughter. He had at least one reasonable legal alternative: he could have struggled on, with what was unquestionably a difficult situation, by helping Tracy to live and by minimizing her pain as much as possible. [Latimer] might have done so by using a feeding tube to improve her health and allow her to take more effective pain medication, or he might have relied on the group home that Tracy stayed at just before her death.
>
> [Latimer] may well have thought the prospect of struggling on [would be] unbearably sad and demanding. It was a human response that this alternative was unappealing. *But it was a reasonable legal alternative that the law requires a person to pursue before he can claim the defence of necessity. [Latimer] was aware of this alternative but rejected it* [emphasis added].

PROPORTIONALITY

We come now to the third factor in the necessity defence: *proportionality* — weighing the wrong done against the benefit obtained. The Court assumed that this aspect of the defence might apply to Latimer. But, it found that the facts proved by him simply were inadequate. The Court stated:

> Assuming for the sake of analysis only that necessity could provide a defence to homicide, there

would have to be a harm that was seriously comparable in gravity to death (the harm inflicted). In this case, there was no risk of such harm. The "harm avoided" in [Latimer's] situation was, compared to death, completely disproportionate. The harm inflicted in this case was ending a life; that harm was immeasurably more serious than the pain resulting from Tracy's operation which Mr. Latimer sought to avoid. Killing a person — in order to relieve the suffering produced by a medically manageable physical or mental condition — is not a proportionate response to the harm represented by the non-life-threatening suffering resulting from that condition.

The Court left no doubt as to its findings:

We conclude that there was no air of reality to any of the three requirements for necessity. As noted earlier, if the trial judge concludes that even one of the requirements had no air of reality, the defence should not be left to the jury. Here, the trial judge was correct to remove the defence from the jury. In considering the defence of necessity, we must remain aware of the need to respect the life, dignity, and equality of all the individuals affected by the act in question. The fact that the victim in this case was disabled rather than able-bodied does not affect our conclusion that the three requirements for the defence of necessity had no air of reality here.

NO SURPRISE TO THE DEFENCE

The trial court's rejection of the necessity defence, said the Supreme Court of Canada, should not have come as a surprise to the Latimer defence. The necessity defence had been rejected in the first Latimer trial, and that ruling was affirmed by a unanimous Saskatchewan Court of Appeal.

The Supreme Court stated in *Latimer*:

> It was hardly a surprise that the trial judge eventually removed the defence of necessity. The decision did not ambush [Latimer], nor should it have caught him unaware. The trial judge in the first Latimer case had removed the defence, and the Court of Appeal in *Latimer* ... unanimously agreed.
>
> The ruling was obvious: there was no air of reality to even one of the three requirements for necessity. In discussing his decision to delay ruling on necessity until after closing [arguments], the tenor of the trial judge's comments makes it apparent that he was highly skeptical that the defence was available. We are of the view that the surprise here, if any, was minimal, and we fail to see the prejudice [to Latimer]. While it is customary and in most instances preferable for the trial judge to rule on the availability of a defence prior to closing addresses to the jury, it cannot be said that the failure to do so here resulted in an unfair trial.

CHALLENGE QUESTION

STANDARD: OBJECTIVE OR SUBJECTIVE?

For the defence of necessity to apply in a criminal case, is it enough that an accused honestly believes that each of these three elements apply: imminent peril, no reasonable legal alternative to disobeying the law, and proportionality?

It is not enough that an accused subjectively believes the three elements of the necessity defence apply to him/her. In *Latimer*, the Supreme Court of Canada said that there must be an objective belief basis for each of the three elements. The reason: Society has an expectation of "appropriate and normal resistance [by the accused] to pressure."

As to the first two factors of the necessity defence (imminent peril and no reasonable legal alternative to committing the offence), the Court said that the accused would be required to show the objective facts to support the claim. But, the accused would also be permitted to have the court take into account his/her individual situation and character. The Court stated:

> While an accused's perceptions of the surrounding facts may be highly relevant in determining whether his conduct should be excused, those perceptions remain relevant only so long as they are reasonable. The accused person must, at the time of the act, honestly believe, on reasonable grounds, that he faces a situation of imminent peril that leaves no reasonable legal alternative open.

There must be a reasonable basis for the accused's beliefs and actions, but it would be proper to take into account circumstances that legitimately affect the accused person's ability to evaluate his situation. The test cannot be a subjective one, and the accused who argues that he perceived imminent peril without an alternative would only succeed with the defence of necessity if his belief was reasonable given his circumstances and attributes....

THE THIRD ELEMENT: PROPORTIONALITY

Proportionality, said the Court, must be measured on a purely objective standard. To do otherwise would violate "fundamental principles of criminal law." The reason: "Evaluating the nature of an act is fundamentally a determination reflecting society's values as to what is appropriate and what represents a transgression."

There is a threshold at which a person must be expected to suffer the harm rather than break the law. This is a *moral judgment*. But, a valuable aid in coming to judgment is to *objectively* compare the harm inflicted by the accused against the benefit arising from the action taken. The Court stated:

The evaluation of the seriousness of the harms must be objective. A subjective evaluation of the competing harms would, by definition, look at the matter from the perspective of the accused person who seeks to avoid harm, usually to himself. The proper perspective, however, is an objective one, since evaluating the gravity of the act is a matter of community standards infused with constitutional considerations (such as, in this case, the section 15(1) equality rights of the disabled [under the Charter of Rights and Freedoms]). We conclude that the proportionality requirement must be determined on a purely objective standard.

CAN MURDER EVER BE PROPORTIONAL?

Is it possible, as a matter of law, for murder ever to be a proportional response within the meaning of the necessity defence? Probably not. The Supreme Court of Canada stated:

The third requirement for the necessity defence is proportionality; it requires the trial judge to consider, as a question of law rather than fact, whether the harm avoided was proportionate to the harm inflicted.

It is difficult, at the conceptual level, to imagine a circumstance in which the proportionality requirement could be met for a homicide. We leave open, if and until it arises, the question of whether the proportionality requirement could be met in a homicide situation.

In England, the defence of necessity is probably not available for homicide.... The Law

Reform Commission of Canada has suggested the defence should not be available for a person who intentionally kills or seriously harms another person: *Report on Recodifying Criminal Law* (1987), at p. 36. American jurisdictions are divided on this question, with a number of them denying the necessity defence for murder....

(As noted, the Court assumed in law that this aspect of the defence might be sought by Latimer. Based on the facts, however, the Court found Latimer had absolutely no objective basis for making such a claim.)

THE RIGHT TO THE OPPORTUNITY FOR JURY NULLIFICATION

The second major ground for appeal heard by the Supreme Court of Canada in the Latimer case was that Latimer was denied the opportunity of *jury nullification*. In effect, jury nullification means that the jury, regardless of the evidence, chooses not to apply the law and instead acquits the defendant.

But, how can this be? Isn't the function of the jury to weigh the facts in accordance with the law as given to it by the judge, and then return a verdict? This is what the Court said of jury nullification in *Latimer*:

Jury nullification is a situation where a jury knowingly chooses not to apply the law and acquits a defendant regardless of the strength of the evidence against him. Jury nullification is an unusual concept within the criminal law, since it effectively acknowledges that it may occur that the jury elects in the rarest of cases not to apply the law. The explanation seems to be that, on some occasions, oppression will result either from a harsh law or from a harsh application of a law.

This Court has referred to the jury's power to nullify as "the citizen's ultimate protection against oppressive laws and the oppressive enforcement of the law" and it has characterized the jury nullification power as a "safety valve" for exceptional cases.... At the same time, however, Chief Justice Dickson warned that "recognizing this reality [that a jury may nullify] is a far cry from suggesting that counsel may encourage a jury to ignore a law they do not support or to tell a jury that it has a right to do so."

In effect, the Court stated that juries, on their own, may ignore the law. They may ignore their sworn duty to apply the law fairly to the facts. But, this is not the same as bestowing on the accused a right to have jury nullification. The Court stated:

An accused is entitled to a fair trial, including the presumption of innocence, the duty of the Crown to prove guilt beyond a reasonable doubt, and the ability to make full answer and defence.

The accused is not entitled to a trial that increases the possibility of jury nullification. If the trial of the accused has not been unfair and no miscarriage of justice has occurred, the accused cannot succeed on an argument that due to some departure from the norm by the trial judge, his chances of jury nullification are lessened [emphasis added].

NULLIFICATION APPLIED TO LATIMER

Latimer argued that if the jury had been allowed to consider the defence of necessity — even though it was at best marginal in substance — it might have decided to nullify. And, indeed, if the trial judge had not suggested to the jury that it might have some input into the sentence when, in fact, this was precluded by the law (at least as to a minimum sentence), it might have decided to nullify.

The Supreme Court of Canada rejected both arguments:

1. It was for the trial judge to determine whether there was an "air of reality" to the defence of necessity. And, for the reasons set out earlier in this chapter, the ruling was that there was simply no basis to the claimed defence. This was a matter which the Supreme Court of Canada reviewed in considerable depth, as described, sustaining the ruling of the trial court judge. In effect, there was no duty of the trial judge to put before a jury a question of law that had no basis in the facts that had been proved.

2. But, what is to be said about the failure of the trial judge to allow the jury to comment on any possible sentence? Was it misleading for the trial judge to suggest, in response to a jury question, that there would be the opportunity for comment? After all, in law, the only matter upon which the jury might have had any input was whether the minimum sentence of ten years imprisonment should have been increased. Latimer argued that if the jury knew they could not input into a lesser sentence, then there might have been a greater opportunity for jury nullification. Again, the Court rejected the argument. It stated:

> The rule in Canada is that guilt is for the jury to determine, while sentencing is left to the trial judge. That long-standing approach is sensible as

a trial judge will obviously have more knowledge on both the acceptable range of sentences for the particular offence and the principles of sentencing. The jury's role is to determine on the facts whether the evidence establishes guilt. There is no reason to depart from the general rule.

It may seem odd that the jury, without knowing the penalty, could be blind to the consequences of its conclusions, but that fact is both appropriate and desirable when one takes into account the risk that the jury could be influenced — whether towards acquitting or convicting — on the basis of the sentence. That logic applies with the same force when the prescribed penalty is a statutory minimum.

The fact that a convicted person will be subject to a pre-designated minimum sentence should not influence the jury's consideration of the question of guilt. [Latimer] suggests that the jury was less likely to nullify because it was not explicitly told of the mandatory minimum sentence. The question of whether the jury would have been more likely to acquit if informed of the mandatory minimum sentence — however interesting its speculation may be — cannot be the basis for a requirement that the jury be informed of the penalty consequent on conviction.

A CHARTER "RIGHT"

More broadly, Latimer claimed what amounted to a Charter right — that is, a constitutional right — to the opportunity for jury nullification. He did this under section 7 of the Charter which affords the right to life, liberty, and security of the person except to the extent the government curtails such rights "in accordance with the principles of fundamental justice." The Court added:

> Latimer's second argument is a broad one, that the accused person has some right to jury nullification. How could there be any such "right"? As a matter of logic and principle, the law cannot encourage jury nullification. When it occurs, it may be appropriate to acknowledge that occurrence. But ... saying that jury nullification may occur is distant from deliberately allowing the defence to argue it before a jury or letting a judge raise the possibility of nullification in his or her instructions to the jury.
>
> [Latimer] concedes as much, but advances some right, on the part of the accused person, to a jury whose power to nullify is not undermined. He suggests the right to a fair trial under section 7 of the *Charter* encompasses this entitlement. [Latimer] submits that there is a jury power to nullify, and it would be unconstitutional to undermine that power.

The Court stated:

> We reject that proposition. [Latimer] cannot legitimately rely on a broad right to jury nullification. In this case, the trial did not become unfair simply because the trial judge undermined the jury's power [in fact, though not in law] to nullify. In most if not all cases, jury nullification will not be a valid factor in analyzing trial fairness for the accused. Guarding against jury nullification is a desirable and legitimate exercise for a trial judge; in fact, a judge is required to take steps to ensure

that the jury will apply the law properly.... Steps taken by a trial judge to guard against jury nullification should not, on that basis alone, prejudice the accused person.

AN EXAMPLE OF JURY NULLIFICATION: SPECIAL CIRCUMSTANCES?

Ted and Rose Bates, immigrants from England, had lived in Saskatchewan for about nineteen years when, as a result of the Depression, their savings were wiped out. In the spring of 1932, they were forced to sell their butcher shop in Glidden for $450. But, the sale price was never paid.

The Bateses moved to Vancouver and opened another store. That, too, failed. They were at the end of their economic rope. They were too proud to seek public charity, but they had no choice. There was no money for food or shelter.

The B.C. government, like that of other provinces, placed the burden of welfare to a great extent on local authorities, that is, on the cities and towns. And, the local governments, with few exceptions, required those seeking help to go back to their home towns. The Bateses found no help in Vancouver.

ONE-WAY TICKETS

The Bateses were forced to return to Saskatchewan — with the help of one-way train tickets provided by the Salvation Army. In Saskatoon, officials repeated what they had told the Bateses earlier: If they wanted help, they would have to return to their home town of Glidden. The couple, as a matter of pride, could not do this. The Saskatoon officials gave them coupons for a weekend at a local hotel and two meals a day. But, their help ended when the weekend was over.

The couple decided to end their lives, and that of their son, Jack. Rose Bates pawned her jewelry for $10. With the money, they rented a car and bought gas with a portion of what remained. On Monday, they drove to the town of Perdue. There was only enough money left to buy three quarts of gas from a farmer. They parked the car that night at the rear of a public school.

Jack sat quietly in the back seat, reading from two books: *Chester Gump at Silver Creek Ranch* and *Mickey Mouse: The Mail Pilot*. Ted Bates took a tube, attached it to the exhaust, and then brought it to the window of the car. The car was turned on. The window was opened only enough to leave room for the hose. The couple waited for death from the carbon monoxide fumes.

A CHILD DIES

There was not enough gas to kill the parents, but there was enough to kill Jack. His parents woke from the stupor caused by the fumes. When they saw what had happened, they tried unsuccessfully to kill themselves through other means. It was in that situation that police found them. The couple were taken to hospital where they recovered.

The residents of Glidden learned of the tragedy. They called a mass meeting, which was put off for a day because of a snowstorm so that neighbouring farmers could attend.

Those attending the meeting drafted a resolution that declared that what happened to the Bateses was a "direct result of the Depression." They urged the government in Ottawa to take full charge of relief. That plea was denied. However, the meeting did raise money for Jack's funeral.

THE TRIAL

The Crown laid criminal charges against the Bateses and brought them to trial one hundred days after the death of their son. Crown

Counsel argued that responsibility for Jack's death rested with his parents. The jury, consisting of local residents, listened to the Crown's case, and they found the Bateses not guilty. At that point, the crowded courtroom broke out in applause. In effect, the jury's verdict was nullification of the law.

LENIENCY FOR HOMICIDE — THE U.S.A.

In 2009 Jonathan Turley, a professor of public interest law and a practising criminal defence lawyer, wrote that hundreds of children were believed to have died in the United States from 1984 to 2009 after faith-healing parents denied them medical attention to end their sickness or protect their lives.

In law, these parents could have been charged with criminal neglect or — even as with Robert Latimer — murder. But, Turley said, "when parents say the neglect was an article of faith, courts routinely hand down lighter sentences. Faithful neglect has not been used as a criminal defense, but the claim is surprisingly effective in achieving more lenient sentencing...."

Turley cited as an example a case arising in the state of Wisconsin, which has under its child abuse laws statutory exemption regarding child neglect that is based on faith. Leilani and Dale Neumann were sentenced for allowing their eleven-year-old daughter, Madeline, to die in 2008 from an undiagnosed but treatable form of diabetes.

The Neumanns were affiliated with a faith-healing church called Unleavened Bread Ministries. They prayed with other members while Madeline died. They could have received twenty-five years in prison. Instead, the court emphasized their religious beliefs and gave them each six months in jail (to be served one month a year) and ten years probation. They were allowed to keep their remaining children.

During their sentencing, Marathon County Circuit Court Judge Vincent Howard said the Neumanns were "very good people raising their family who made a bad decision, a reckless decision." He then gently encouraged them to remember that "God probably works through other people, some of them doctors."

Turley stated:

> The advocacy group Children's Health Care Is a Legal Duty estimates that roughly 300 children have died in the United States since 1975 because care was withheld. When such parents appear in court, they often insist that they love their children and their God — an argument that receives a sympathetic hearing from judges and prosecutors.
>
> While defendants generally show contrition for their actions, the Neumanns remained unrepentant about not calling emergency personnel until after Madeline stopped breathing. Leilani Neumann said: "I do not regret trusting truly in the Lord for my daughter's health." Dale Neumann told the court: "I am guilty of trusting my Lord's wisdom completely.... Guilty of asking for heavenly intervention. Guilty of following Jesus Christ when the whole world does not understand. Guilty of obeying my God."

THE LATIMER SENTENCE: CRUEL AND UNUSUAL PUNISHMENT?

Recall that the trial court judge imposed a "constitutional exemption" and sentenced Robert Latimer to one year in prison and one year of probation confined to his farm. He did this on the grounds that the ten-year minimum sentence for second degree murder, as applied to Latimer, would have been cruel and unusual punishment, which is prohibited under section 12 of the Charter of Rights and Freedoms, part of the Constitution of Canada and, as such, the supreme law of the land.

However, the Saskatchewan Court of Appeal reversed the trial court on this point and imposed the minimum ten-year sentence without the possibility of parole. It is this question that the Supreme Court of Canada also heard.

The Supreme Court affirmed the judgment of the Court of Appeal: the ten-year sentence as applied to Latimer was not cruel and unusual punishment. We emphasize that Latimer did not question the constitutionality of the minimum-sentence law. What he questioned was the constitutionality of that law as applied to him.

THE TEST

To grant a "constitutional exemption" means, at least in the individual case of Latimer, setting aside a clear law enacted by Parliament. The Court stated that it would not easily overturn such a law. In effect, said the Court, for such a law to be overturned there must be a great difference between the wrong done and the penalty imposed by the law — in this case, the minimum sentence of ten years. Indeed, the difference must be so great as to outrage standards of decency.

The Court stated:

> While the test is one that attributes a great deal of weight to individual circumstances, it should also be stressed that in weighing the section 12 considerations, the court must also consider and defer to the valid legislative objectives underlying the criminal law responsibilities of Parliament....

It will only be on rare and unique occasions
that a court will find a sentence so grossly disproportionate that it violates the provisions of section
12 of the Charter. *The test for determining whether
a sentence is disproportionately long is very properly stringent and demanding. A lesser test would
tend to trivialize the Charter* [emphasis added].

THE TEST APPLIED

In effect, there were two parts to the test applied to Latimer:

1. How did the sentence affect him? For example, would a sentence of ten years have much meaning in terms of the likelihood that Latimer again would commit a similar crime?
2. What meaning should be given to Parliament's goal in setting a ten-year minimum sentence? Would such a sentence
   serve to set an example, or to deter others?

The Court stated that Latimer had been found guilty of the
most serious crime: the subjective, intentional taking of the life of
another. In effect, there is no difference between first degree and
second degree murder, said the Court, except the term of imprisonment. It is against this "reality" that the Court weighed the facts
individual to Latimer. In doing so, it considered both "aggravating
and mitigating" circumstances.

The following was the Court's reasoning in ruling that the ten-
year sentence did not violate section 12 of the Charter:

On the one hand, we must give due consideration
to Mr. Latimer's initial attempts to conceal his
actions, his lack of remorse, his position of trust,
the significant degree of planning and premeditation, and Tracy's extreme vulnerability. On the
other hand, we are mindful of Mr. Latimer's good

character and standing in the community, his tortured anxiety about Tracy's well-being, and his laudable perseverance as a caring and involved parent. Considered together, *we cannot find that the personal characteristics and particular circumstances of this case displace the serious gravity of this offence* [emphasis added].

Finally, this sentence is consistent with a number of valid penological goals and sentencing principles. *Although we would agree that in this case the sentencing principles of rehabilitation, specific deterrence, and protection are not triggered for consideration, we are mindful of the important role that the mandatory minimum sentence plays in denouncing murder.* Denunciation of unlawful conduct is one of the objectives of sentencing recognized in §718 of the Criminal Code [emphasis added].

Furthermore, denunciation becomes much more important in the consideration of sentencing in cases where there is a "high degree of planning and premeditation, and where the offence and its consequences are highly publicized, [so that] like-minded individuals may well be deterred by severe sentences." ... This is particularly so where the victim is a vulnerable person with respect to age, disability, or other similar factors.

ANOTHER APPEAL FOR LATIMER?

The Supreme Court of Canada affirmed the conviction and sentence of Latimer. However, is it possible for him to have that sentence changed after the nation's highest court has ruled? The

Supreme Court of Canada, itself, suggested that there might be another way for Latimer to have his sentence changed: the Royal Prerogative of Mercy (RPM). Through the Crown, power to exercise the RPM is vested in the Governor in Council (i.e. the Federal Cabinet) to grant a pardon or a conditional pardon to any person convicted of an offence.

For our purposes, the relevant provisions of the Criminal Code provide:

> §749(1) Her Majesty may extend the royal mercy to a person who is sentenced to imprisonment under the authority of an Act of Parliament....
>
> (2) The Governor in Council may grant a free pardon or a conditional pardon to any person who has been convicted of an offence.
>
> (3) Where the Governor in Council grants a free pardon to a person, that person shall be deemed thereafter never to have committed the offence in respect of which the pardon was granted....

The Court seemed to suggest that the statutory use of a mandatory minimum sentence, coupled with the facts of the Latimer case, might prompt the government to grant some form of pardon. In this regard, the Court noted that there is "considerable difference of opinion ... on the wisdom of employing minimum sentences from a criminal law policy or penelogical point of view."

But, the decision to grant a pardon of any kind is not a judicial matter. It is a matter of government policy. The Court stated in *Latimer*:

> The prerogative [the grant of a pardon] is a matter for the executive, not the courts. The executive will undoubtedly, if it chooses to consider the matter, examine all of the underlying circumstances surrounding the tragedy of Tracy Latimer

that took place on October 24, 1993, some seven years ago. Since that time, Mr. Latimer has undergone two trials and two appeals to the Court of Appeal for Saskatchewan and this Court, with attendant publicity and consequential agony for him and his family.

CHALLENGE QUESTIONS

FOR THE LATIMER FAMILY: FORCED CHOICE?

Would the agency be able to have a court declare Tracy a ward of the province for the purposes outlined of treatment and convalescence? If the agency were successful, then would it be able to act in effect as Tracy's parents and order the listed procedures to take place?

Suppose that, before her death, a government child welfare agency determined that it would be in Tracy Latimer's best interest: (1) to have a feeding tube inserted into her stomach; (2) to have additional surgeries; and (3) to be cared for during convalescence at a government-run hospital. Assume, further, that the agency was able to prove that without the proposed medical procedures, Tracy's life would be endangered.

However, these were all choices that had been rejected by Tracy's parents. Bear in mind that this is only a hypothetical question. Nothing in the facts relating to the case against Robert Latimer suggested that the medical procedures noted were *required* to save Tracy's life. Rather, the procedures seemed designed to *improve* the quality of her life.

However, having said this, on the basis of the hypothetical question, it is likely that a court would award the
wardship to the agency for a period long enough to do that
which would be reasonably necessary medically to protect
Tracy's life. In asking a court to declare Tracy a ward of the
agency, it follows that a hearing would be given to show the
necessity for the proposed procedures.

It was in *Richard B. v. Children's Aid Society of
Metropolitan Toronto as Official Guardian for Sheena B.,*
[1995] 1 *Supreme Court of Canada Reports* 315 that the
Supreme Court of Canada allowed a wardship to a government agency over an infant whose parents, on religious
grounds, refused blood transfusions for their infant child.
The transfusions were shown by the agency to be necessary
to protect the infant's life.

The start point in analysis is to recognize that no one
may impose medical treatment on another without that
person's consent. Supreme Court of Canada Justice Peter
Cory said: "It should not be forgotten that every patient has
a right to bodily integrity. This encompasses the right to
determine what medical procedures will be accepted and
the extent to which they will be accepted. Everyone has the
right to decide what is to be done to one's own body. This
right includes the right to be free from medical treatment
to which the individual does not consent." (*Ciarlariello v.
Schachter,* [1993] 2 *Supreme Court of Canada Reports* 119,
at 135.)

Parents have the right (and the responsibility) in law
to provide for the necessities (including medical needs) of
their minor children. In *Richard B.,* this right/duty can take
on an interest protected by the Charter. But, it is the life of
the child which is of concern to the Court. Where there has

> been a fair hearing and a judicial decision made in the best
> interest of the child, the Charter interest of the parents will
> be deemed to have been protected.

LATIMER PAROLED

Robert Latimer was fifty-six when he was convicted of second degree murder for killing his severely disabled twelve-year-old daughter, Tracy. After the ten-year mandatory sentence, before becoming eligible for parole, Latimer chose and was granted day parole at a halfway house in Victoria, B.C., in March 2008. Apparently, he chose British Columbia because he could — and did — enroll in a full-time college-level program for training as an electrician.

On December 4, 2009, the National Probation Board allowed an extended leave from December 24, 2009 to January 7, 2010. This allowed Latimer to return to visit his family and farm in Saskatchewan.

On November 29, 2010, Latimer was granted a full parole and was free to return to his home in Saskatchewan.

Latimer continued to express disappointment with the hearings he had received. He said: "If you look at the first trial, that wasn't honest. [The decision of the trial court was overturned, and a new trial ordered on the basis of improper jury selection.] Then they pretty much had to carry it through and make that credible with another trial, which was just as crooked. They won't allow a jury to decide whether it was right or wrong."

He added that he was "haunted" by a reference the Supreme Court of Canada made, saying more effective pain medication could have been given to his daughter. Latimer said his understanding was that his daughter could handle only children's Tylenol.

Latimer held to the view that his jury was not allowed to consider what he saw as the central question in his trial: Was he right or wrong in choosing to end what he saw as his daughter's suffering? The chance, as he saw it, to review that question came up when he sought parole without restrictions to travel outside Canada. Initially, the parole board denied Latimer's application to travel without restrictions (such as reporting to the parole board). On appeal, the agency's appeal board upheld the restriction.

Latimer then appealed to the Federal Court, and his appeal was sustained in part. The court ordered the parole appeal board to reconsider its judgment. Latimer's record, said the court, had nothing in it to indicate that he was a danger and needed to be prevented from freely travelling outside of Canada. (At the time, Latimer was sixty.)

The parole board duly reconsidered its judgment. It found that the condition of reporting to the board should remain. Latimer was "low-risk" in terms of any repeat violation, but a level of risk did remain. The parole board stated: "It is concerning to the board, however, that we read on file that there has been no change in your thinking and level of rationalization which led to the offence. You continue to deny this was a murder and believe what you did was the right thing to do. This represents a level of risk."

There was also a reference to concerns about how the board would manage Latimer's conditions if he were approved for unrestricted travel.

REFERENCES AND FURTHER READING

* Cited by the Supreme Court of Canada.

American Law Institute. *Model Penal Code and Commentaries*, Part I, vol. 2. Philadelphia, PA: 1985.*

Berton, Pierre. *The Great Depression: 1929–1933.* Toronto: McClelland & Stewart, 1990.

Fletcher, George P. *Rethinking Criminal Law.* Boston: Little, Brown and Co., 1978.*

Keyserlingk, E. *"Sanctity of Life or Quality of Life in the Context of Ethics, Medicine and Law. "* Study Paper for the Law Reform Commission of Canada, Protection of Life Project, Ottawa, 1979.*

"Latimer Still Defends Killing Daughter." CBC.ca, February 17, 2011.

Miller, Jeffrey. "N.B. Teen Had Statutory Right to Refuse Transfusions." *The Lawyers Weekly*, July 22, 1994.

"Robert Latimer Granted Full Parole." CTV.ca, November 29, 2010.

"Robert Latimer's out-of-country travel conditions remain, parole board rules." *Canadian Press*, November 17, 2014.

Somerville, M.A. "Pain and Suffering: Medicine and Law." *University of Toronto Law Journal* 36 (1986): 286.*

Spencer, Beverly. "State Can Ensure Children Get Treatment, Says Top Court." *The Lawyers Weekly*, February 17, 1995.

Turley, Jonathan. "When a child dies, faith is no defense. Why do courts give believers a pass?" *Washington Post*, November 15, 2009.

CHAPTER 4

ASSISTED SUICIDE: A "RIGHT" TO DIE?

Is it unlawful to help another person to die? Does it matter that the person seeking such help is in pain and not able to end her/his life with their own hands? Is this really suicide by another name?

Among the questions raised in this chapter are:

- Is the attempt to commit suicide unlawful under the Criminal Code?
- What is physician-assisted suicide?
- What are the medical principles guiding physicians in relation to assisted suicide?

The search for answers takes us to cases where questions of life, death, and the role of law as set by the legislature — embodied in the Charter of Rights and Freedoms and interpreted by the courts — are presented .

The central cases in this chapter are *Rodriguez v. British Columbia (Attorney General)*, [1993] 3 *Supreme Court of Canada Reports* 519, and *Carter v. Canada (Attorney General)*, [2015] *Supreme Court of Canada Reports* 5. In a 5–4 decision in *Rodriguez*, the Supreme Court of Canada upheld Criminal Code provisions prohibiting assisted suicide. Violation of that law then could result in imprisonment of up to fourteen years.

In *Carter*, decided by the Supreme Court twenty-two years after *Rodriguez*, the Court reversed its position. The Carter decision was unanimous. All nine members of the Court accepted the decision in *Carter*. To add greater weight to that acceptance, the ruling was formally announced as the decision of "the Court," not the decision of individual justices.

We will set out the case facts, the law, the arguments, and the results, as well as some of the questions to be considered. We will find that the answers of yesterday may not be the same as the answers needed for today or tomorrow. And that, in turn, may cause us to reflect on the role we want our courts, and perhaps especially the Supreme Court of Canada, to play in resolving questions of life and death. We will also probe more deeply, not just about an increasing role for government, but about what we as individuals can do to address concerns relating to dying and death — conditions affecting all of humanity.

The final chapter of this book sets out just one of those possibilities where law, as such, has only a minimal role to play: palliative care. We will find that the Supreme Court in both the Rodriguez and Carter cases did consider public opinion regarding assisted suicide as it was manifested in law (or the lack of such law). If palliative care were provided, the rate of assisted suicide would diminish, according to Angus Reid, the Canadian polling organization director. We will ask what palliative care can entail and, if it were provided on a national basis, to what extent it would it obviate the need for — or at least the need in the same degree — for assisted suicide. In part, this will lead us to a return to the facts of *Rodriguez* and *Carter*.

THE FACTS OF THE RODRIGUEZ CASE

At forty-two, Sue Rodriguez, a resident of British Columbia, was married and had an eight-year-old son. She had amyotrophic lateral sclerosis (ALS), an illness commonly known as Lou Gehrig's disease, for which there is no known cure.

ALS is a disease of the motor neurons of the brain and spinal cord. Motor neurons are nerve cells that control the muscles operating the body. With ALS, the nerve cells die and the muscle units they control weaken and shrink. However, other parts of the brain system, such as those controlling sensation and reasoning, are not affected by the disease. The average life expectancy following a diagnosis of ALS is between two and three years.

Rodriguez made it clear that she wanted to live a full life as long as possible. When it no longer became possible to have quality in her life, she wanted to be able to end it at a time and place of her choosing.

The issue was not that she might lack the will to commit suicide. Indeed, Canada had eliminated from the Criminal Code both the offence of suicide and attempted suicide. Rather, Rodriguez feared that physically she might not be able to end her life by herself. The final stage of her disease would deny her the use of her arms and legs. Indeed, she would lose even the power to breathe without the assistance of a ventilator. To end her life, at a point of her choosing, she would need help. And, the provider of such help would find himself/herself guilty on conviction of the crime of assisted suicide. (This assumes that the "provider" could be identified and her/his role proved.)

Section 241 of the Criminal Code provides:

> Every one who
> (a) counsels a person to commit suicide, or
> (b) aids or abets a person to commit suicide,
> whether suicide ensues or not, is guilty of an

indictable offence and liable to imprisonment for a term not exceeding fourteen years.

Note that the sweep of the law is broad. To fall within its meaning, it is not necessary that the individual counselled commits suicide. It is enough that that person is counselled to commit suicide. For example, under the Criminal Code, a doctor sought out by Rodriguez could not "advise" the mixtures she might take to end her life.

Rodriguez did seek the promise of help from two British Columbia physicians. But they refused, in part because of fear of prosecution under the Criminal Code. At least in theory, she also could have been prosecuted under section 241 for seeking aid to commit suicide.

Rodriguez argued that section 241 was unconstitutional — in violation of the Charter of Rights and Freedoms. As such, she asked the Court, in effect, to nullify the statute. In support of her position, she cited these Charter provisions:

§7. Everyone has the right to life, liberty and security of the person and the right not to be deprived thereof except in accordance with the principles of fundamental justice.

§12. Everyone has the right not to be subjected to any cruel and unusual treatment or punishment.

§15. (1) Every individual is equal before and under the law and has the right to the equal protection and equal benefit of the law without discrimination and, in particular, without discrimination based on race, national or ethnic origin, colour, religion, sex, age or mental or physical disability.

RODRIGUEZ'S CHARTER CHALLENGE
IN BRITISH COLUMBIA

Sue Rodriguez did not begin her court challenge in the Supreme Court of Canada. Few persons do. Indeed, it is safe to say that often years may pass from the start of a case until the matter reaches the Supreme Court. And, even then, the odds are that the Court will not hear the case, as the Court will deny any case that it believes is not of special public importance.

Rodriguez had perhaps only months left in her life and any court challenge, almost by definition, requires time and patience. Still, she sought and obtained legal help through the British Columbia Civil Liberties Association, which brought her challenge to the lower courts of British Columbia.

We will pick up the litigation in Rodriguez's appeal from the British Columbia Court of Appeal. We will find that the arguments and decision in some important ways parallel that of the ruling of the Supreme Court of Canada.

The heart of Rodriguez's argument was that she had a Charter right to control her own body. She sought a declaration of that right with particular reference to section 7 of the Charter which states: "Everyone has the right to life, liberty and security of the person and the right not to be deprived thereof except in accordance with the principles of fundamental justice."

In this regard, she pointed, by way of example, to section 15 of the Charter that, among other things, prohibits discrimination on the basis of physical disability. Individuals without the disability of ALS would not violate the Criminal Code if they committed suicide. Rodriguez, on the other hand, was denied that right. To repeat, her disability would not allow her to commit suicide.

This is how Rodriguez presented her request to the appellate court through her lawyers:

[She] does not wish to face the indignity which will accompany being forced to endure life in such a condition and fears that she will be unable to cope with what will surely be a mentally agonizing death.

She wishes to have the option of committing suicide in the event that [her] remaining life becomes completely unbearable.

[She] wishes to have a physician assist her to commit suicide, although she proposes that she herself commit the final act by technological means which do not require her to swallow pills.

Her Charter argument was rejected by the B.C. Court of Appeal.

THE DECISION OF THE BRITISH COLUMBIA COURT OF APPEAL

By a 2–1 vote, Rodriguez's claim was denied by the Court of Appeal. Each of the three justices of the appellate court wrote an opinion. Justices H.A. Hollinrake and Patricia Proudfoot wrote the majority opinions, and Chief Justice Allan McEachern wrote a forty-three-page dissent.

THE MAJORITY OPINION OF JUSTICE HOLLINRAKE

Justice Hollinrake wrote that human dignity is a part of what goes into the "security of the person," within the meaning of section 7 of the Charter. To deny Rodriguez the opportunity for assisted suicide would deprive her of that security of the person.

However, that is not the end of the matter. That Charter right comes into play when one is deprived of the security of the person contrary to the principles of fundamental justice. The question then is whether section 241 of the Criminal Code deprived Rodriguez of the security of her person contrary to the principles of fundamental justice. The answer, said Justice Hollinrake, is found by asking how a democratic society historically has treated assisted suicide.

Justice Hollinrake could find nothing in the history of Parliament that indicated any intent to end or soften the substance of section 241. The prohibition against aiding suicide, he said, had been part of Canadian criminal law since 1892. Further, when Parliament in 1972 removed the provision in the Criminal Code against attempted suicide — that is, where one attempts to take her/his life alone — section 241 was left intact.

As to the views of doctors concerning assisted suicide, Justice Hollinrake concluded that there was a history of opposition to the practice of physician-assisted suicide. Here is an example of the role of opinion in shaping policy. In this instance, it is the opinion of medical doctors. Justice Hollinrake stated:

> The Canadian Medical Association, the British Medical Association, the American Medical Association and the World Medical Association all condemn the practice of active euthanasia [from Greek, meaning *good death*] and physician-assisted suicide.
>
> However, the medical practice of withdrawing treatment to alleviate pain is acceptable to the profession. The [reasoning] behind the drawing of this distinction seems to be one based on intent.
>
> The withdrawing of treatment is to lessen suffering, which is consistent with the Hippocratic Oath [an ancient code of ethics, the principles of which are still pledged by medical students on their graduation]. Active euthanasia [or mercy

killing] by the physician or by the patient with the doctor's assistance, is to cause death, which runs against the fundamental intuition of medical training. It must be noted that these are the governing bodies of physicians which take this stand.

There is a line, said Justice Hollinrake, between easing the pain of a person facing certain death (called palliative care) that might even hasten death, and intentionally causing death. For Parliament to draw such a line, Justice Hollinrake said, would not violate the principles of fundamental justice.

THE MAJORITY OPINION OF JUSTICE PROUDFOOT
Justice Proudfoot examined section 7 of the Charter both as to the procedure and the substance of what Rodriguez sought. First, as to the procedure, she found that it would make "bad law" to allow Rodriguez to seek a shield for an unnamed person who might violate section 241. Such a person then might never be a defendant in either civil or criminal proceedings. In effect, Rodriguez's action was not so much for her as for others not before the court — namely, it would seem, the views of the people of Canada.

Second, Justice Proudfoot stated that, in any event, a single case was hardly the place to determine the views of the people of Canada. To her the questions involved were better left to Parliament. She stated:

In my view, leaving aside the legal and procedural [questions], the broad religious, ethical, moral and social issues implicit in the merits of this case are not suited for [judgment] by a court on the evidence of a single individual.

On the material available to us, we are in no position to assess the consensus in Canada with respect to assisted suicide. That is a matter more suitable to Parliament with all the means of inquiry at its disposal. I would leave to Parliament the responsibility of taking the pulse of the nation. I am opposed to the court assuming that role and responsibility by the device of formulating a new cause of action, a new procedure and a new remedy.

CHIEF JUSTICE MCEACHERN'S DISSENT

There was a detailed dissent from Chief Justice McEachern who said that the common law of assisted suicide had shown a "fairly recent, enlightened medical-jurisprudential trend towards greater humanity and sensitivity towards the awful problems of terminally ill citizens."

(We will dwell at somewhat greater length on the dissent of the chief justice, partly because of its detail and partly because it framed a part of the dissent for four members of the Supreme Court of Canada on review of the Rodriguez case. And, it should be added that, in no small measure, it brought into sharp relief the limitations the court saw for itself — limitations that might only be more meaningfully addressed by the legislature.)

Palliative care might include the right of mentally competent patients to decline medical assistance, to reject care that might save their lives, or to order life-saving machinery to be turned off. But the chief justice acknowledged that this is different than having a physician take positive action to end a person's life. The Criminal Code, through section 241, could hold liable both the physician and the patient asking the doctor's help for assisted suicide.

The result was that the common law offered no hope for Rodriguez. Her only recourse, in law, said the chief justice, was the Charter and a broad interpretation of the rights included under the headings of life and death. Rodriguez had argued that such subjects included the quality and dignity of life, under the Charter headings of protection of the individual and his/her liberty.

Chief Justice McEachern wrote: "It would be wrong, in my view, to judge this case as a contest between life and death. *The Charter is not concerned only with the fact of life, but also with the quality and dignity of life. In my view, death and the way we die is a part of life itself* [emphasis added]."

Chief Justice McEachern supported this finding principally through reliance on *The Queen v. Morgentaler* [1988] 1 *Supreme Court of Canada Reports* 30, which included abortions as part of health care and, specifically, passages highlighting the flexibility of the protection afforded by the "liberty" and "security of the person" components of section 7 of the Charter.

If women have the right to control their bodies and make fundamental decisions about themselves, he said, then surely all persons, subject to controls, should be able to make provision to end their own needless suffering.

To Chief Justice McEachern, a surface violation of both these elements of section 7 arises when the state imposes prohibitions that have the effect of prolonging the physical and psychological suffering of a person.

FUNDAMENTAL JUSTICE

Chief Justice McEachern asked whether this denial of a terminally ill person's rights under section 7 had been done in accordance with the principles of *fundamental justice* — a condition imposed by section 7.

For all the members of the British Columbia Court of Appeal, including the chief justice, there was the question of just who would be covered by its decision. Sue Rodriguez was not speaking for a class of persons — for all those who were terminally ill. She was speaking for herself. Justice Proudfoot made that fact an important part of her opinion. She would have narrowed the effect of the decision in terms of remedy to Rodriguez alone, because she alone was before the court seeking relief.

At the same time, it was not satisfactory to Chief Justice McEachern that the court should wait for Parliament to act before relief could be granted. For him, there was no real Parliamentary guidance that might be used as precedent. It was "interesting" but not very useful to note, he said, that Parliament had removed the "traditional" common law prohibition on suicide.

Perhaps, however, there was guidance to be found in the law relating to palliative care — that is, medical care to ease pain in dying. How far removed is such physician action from positive assistance to a competent (lucid) terminally ill person to end his or her life? How could this kind of assistance be squared with the mandate of section 7 of the Charter requirement of fundamental justice?

Chief Justice McEachern concluded that section 7 was enacted to support the value of human dignity and individual control over his/her body, so long as such action does not harm others. In logic and law, he said, any provision that imposes a period of senseless physical and psychological suffering upon someone who is shortly to die anyway cannot conform with any principle of fundamental justice.

Finding a violation of section 7 was not the end of the matter. The chief justice would have been bound to allow the violation if it met the conditions of section 1 of the Charter — that is, if the violation was one which could be justified in a free and democratic society. This was no easy task.

The chief justice was sensitive to the fact that only a single person, Sue Rodriguez, appeared as a party before the court. She did indeed raise serious general issues. But, her concern was personal. As such, this allowed the chief justice to avoid passing upon the constitutionality of section 241. His focus was on section 241 and how it affected Rodriguez. In that context, to repeat, he found section 241 in violation of the Charter.

What the chief justice did was fashion a remedy, directly tailored to Rodriguez, just as the Charter through section 24(1) allows. The section states: "Anyone whose rights or freedoms, as guaranteed by this Charter, have been infringed or denied may apply to a court of competent jurisdiction to obtain such remedy as the court considers appropriate and just in the circumstances."

(In so doing, the chief justice left open the possibility that the guidelines for Rodriguez might be applied by others similarly situated.)

GUIDELINES SET OUT BY THE CHIEF JUSTICE

The guidelines or conditions that Rodriguez would have had to meet were as follows:

- Rodriguez had to be mentally competent to make a decision to end her own life. This competence must to be certified in writing by a treating physician and by an independent psychiatrist who have examined her not more than twenty-four hours before arrangements are put in place which would permit her to end her life. Such arrangements must be carried out while one of the physicians actually is present with her.
- The medical certificates must do more than say she is competent. They must also state that, in the opinion of the physicians, she truly desires to end her life, and that she has reached that decision of her own free will without pressure or influence from any source.
- The physicians must also state the following: (a) She is terminally ill and near death. There is no hope for her recovery. (b) She is, or but for her present medication would be, suffering unbearable physical pain or severe psychological distress. (c) The physicians have informed her, and she understands that she has a

continuing right to change her mind about terminating her life. (d) The physicians must also state when, in their opinion, she would likely die (i) if palliative were to be administered to her, or (ii) if palliative care were not given to her.

- Not less than three full days before she is examined by a psychiatrist for the purpose of preparing a certificate of the kind described, the local coroner must be notified. The coroner, or the person named by him or her, may be present at the examination to be sure the patient means to end her life, and is competent to do so.

- One of the two physicians who examined her must continue to re-examine her each day after arrangements are put in place to ensure that she does not indicate any change of mind in terms of ending her life.

- No one may assist her to commit suicide after thirty-one days from the date of the first certificate. And, any arrangements that had been put in place before that time for her to commit suicide are to be discontinued.

- The actual causing of death shall be the act of Rodriguez, herself, and not that of another.

The chief justice said: "These conditions have been prepared in some haste because of the urgency of [Rodriguez's] circumstances, and I would not wish judges in subsequent applications to regard them other than as guidelines."

THE SUPREME COURT OF CANADA DECIDES

The Supreme Court of Canada decided soon after the British Columbia Court of Appeal ruling that it would hear the case of Sue Rodriguez in what amounted to a special early session of the Court on May 20, 1993.

About four and a half hours were given over for oral argument on the appeals presented. The issue was not one only between Rodriguez and the Crown, that is, the Attorneys General of Canada and British Columbia. The issues went beyond what the dissent of Chief Justice McEachern would have allowed (namely, a remedy limited to Rodriguez).

Seven organizations, each claiming a special interest in the issues raised in the Rodriguez case, asked for and were granted the right to intervene, that is, to place their positions before the Court. These groups included: the British Columbia Coalition of People with Disabilities, Dying with Dignity, the Right to Die Society of Canada, the Coalition of Provincial Organizations of the Handicapped, the Pro-Life Society of British Columbia, the Pacific Physicians for Life Society, the Canadian Conference of Catholic Bishops, the Evangelical Fellowship of Canada, and People in Equal Participations Inc.

Having decided to give Rodriguez an early hearing might have signalled an intent, on the part of the Court, to come down with an early decision. Such was not the case. The issues simply were too complex. This can be seen in reading the transcript of the oral arguments. And, it certainly comes through in all of the Court's opinions.

The majority opinion was written by Justice John Sopinka for five of the nine justices. There were three dissenting opinions: the dissent of then Justice Beverley McLachlin (later to become chief justice of the Court) in which Justice Claire L'Heureux-Dubé concurred; the dissent of then Chief Justice Antonio Lamer; and the dissent of Justice Peter Cory (who accepted the reasoning of the other dissents).

It is true that the decision of the Supreme Court of Canada states the law. Sometimes, however, there are questions as to the scope of the majority decision. For Sue Rodriguez, on the facts as applied to her, the Court's decision was clear: Her appeal was denied. Left unresolved by the Court majority was what Parliament might do within the bounds of the Charter to decriminalize assisted suicide.

THE MAJORITY OPINION OF JUSTICE SOPINKA

Justice Sopinka said that there was nothing in the Charter which required the outcome sought by Rodriguez. And he further stated that there were a number of "serious concerns" that the majority had in terms of the relief she sought:

- If the Court were to grant what Sue Rodriguez asked, said Justice Sopinka, it would recognize a "constitutional right to legally assisted suicide beyond that of any country in the Western world, beyond any serious proposal for reform in the Western world, and beyond the claim made in this very case."
- There were no real controls over the assistance sought by Rodriguez. Rather, a judge alone would decide, and his or her decision would look at the so-called controls only as guides that need not be followed in a particular case. There would be no review by another court of that judge's action unless a charge were brought after the suicide against the person who assisted in violation of the Criminal Code (section 241).
- There is no obligation on the part of any physician to provide a patient with suicide assistance. And, even if there were such a requirement, it is likely that "many doctors will refuse to assist, leaving open the potential for the growth of a macabre specialty in this area of Dr. Kevorkian and his suicide machine."

(Dr. Jack Kevorkian, an American medical pathologist, assisted twenty people to commit suicide with the aid of a device he constructed. He was later tried and found guilty of second degree murder in the death of the last person he helped to commit suicide. He was sentenced to serve ten to twenty-five years in a maximum security prison. Paroled after eight years, he died in 2011.)

SECTION 7 RIGHTS

Justice Sopinka examined section 7 of the Charter, which he believed to be the legal foundation of Rodriguez's strongest argument. It provides: "Everyone has the right to life, liberty and security of the person and the right not to be deprived thereof except in accordance with the principles of fundamental justice."

Sue Rodriguez argued that section 241(b) of the Criminal Code stopped anyone from helping her to end her life when she was no longer able to do so on her own. This denied her, she said, both her liberty and security of the person under section 7 of the Charter — rights that had important meaning for her:

- the right to live "with the inherent dignity of a human person" her remaining life;
- the right to control what happened to her body while she was living;
- the right to be free from government interference in making basic personal decisions about the final stages of her life.

Justice Sopinka said the first two rights listed deal with *liberty and security of the person* under section 7 of the Charter. He wrote:

> The effect of the prohibition in [section 241] is to prevent [Rodriguez] from having assistance to commit suicide when she no longer is able to do so on her own. She fears that she will be required to live until the deterioration of her disease is

such that she will die as a result of choking, suffo-
cation or pneumonia.... She will be totally dependent upon others.

Throughout this time, she will remain mentally competent and able to [understand] all that
is happening to her. Although [medical] care
may be available to ease the pain and other physical discomfort which she will experience, [she]
fears the sedating effects of such drugs and [she]
argues, in any event, that they will not prevent the
psychological and emotional distress which will
result from being in a situation of utter depen-
dence and loss of dignity.

The Court majority stated that Rodriguez had a "security
interest" within the meaning of section 7 of the Charter that was
affected by the operation of section 241 of the Criminal Code.
Again, speaking for the Court majority, Justice Sopinka wrote:

That there is a right to choose how one's body will
be dealt with, even in the context of beneficial
medical treatment, has long been recognized by
the common law. To impose medical treatment on
one who refuses it constitutes battery [an unlawful act], and our common law has recognized the
right to demand that medical treatment which
would extend life be withheld or withdrawn.

In my view, these considerations lead to the
conclusion that the prohibition in §241 deprives
[Rodriguez] of autonomy [control] over her person and causes her physical pain and psychological
stress in a manner which [violates] the security of
the person....

A "DEFENCE" FOR VIOLATION?

To say that the security interest of Rodriguez is included within section 7 of the Charter is only the start of the analysis to determine whether that section has been violated. Look again at section 7: "Everyone has the right to life, liberty and security of the person and the right not to be deprived thereof *except in accordance with the principles of fundamental justice* [emphasis added]."

Put somewhat differently, there would not have been a violation of section 7 if Rodriguez had been denied her right to security of the person in accordance with a principle of fundamental justice.

But, what is a denial of fundamental justice?

Justice Sopinka said that not every law that fails to give respect to human dignity is a denial of fundamental justice. To rule otherwise would make the language of section 7 repetitive. That is, to so rule would make every denial of security of the person a denial of a principle of fundamental justice. Speaking for the Court majority, he stated that Parliament must have intended to do more than simply repeat the language of section 7. "This interpretation," he said, "would equate security of the person with the principle of fundamental justice and [make] the latter redundant [repetitive and therefore without meaning]."

The Court majority said that the principle of fundamental justice related to protecting society. This, in turn, means that human dignity must be balanced with the protection of society

STATE INTEREST IN ASSISTED SUICIDE

Justice Sopinka found a strong state interest in other parts of the Criminal Code — an interest that reflects an important value: the sanctity of human life. He wrote:

> [Section 241] has as its purpose the protection of
> the vulnerable who might be induced in moments

of weakness to commit suicide. This purpose is grounded in the state interest in protecting life and reflects the policy of the state that human life should not [be lessened] by allowing life to be taken.

This policy finds expression not only in the provisions of the Criminal Code which prohibit murder and other violent acts against others [despite] the consent of the victim, but also in the policy against capital punishment and, until its repeal, attempted suicide. This is not only a policy of the state, however, but is part of our fundamental conception of human life.

Justice Sopinka looked to three areas for policy balance: (1) the history of suicide; (2) medical care at the end of life; and (3) the laws of other countries.

THE HISTORY OF SUICIDE

In reviewing the history of suicide, Justice Sopinka saw an ongoing principle that emphasized the *sanctity of life*. The fact that suicide and attempted suicide were no longer treated as crimes, he said, had more to do with the best way to deal with the problem. A state's concern with preserving life remained.

MEDICAL CARE AT THE END OF LIFE

Justice Sopinka noted several then-recent decisions that permitted patients to withdraw life-support devices or treatments. Yet, he said, this could not be done unless patients clearly understood that their decision probably would cause death.

A decision of the United States Supreme Court was cited: *Cruzan v. Director, Missouri Department of Health, 497 United*

States Supreme Court Reports 261 (1990). In question was the application of the protection of liberty as embodied in the 14th Amendment of the U.S. Constitution to a person in a vegetative state. The U.S. Supreme Court ruled that the state could require compelling evidence that withdrawal of medical treatment was, in fact, what the patient would have requested had she been able to do so.

Neither the Cruzan case nor others, Justice Sopinka wrote, involved the assistance of a third person in ending life. This the courts would have refused. He stated:

> The basis for this [court] refusal is twofold. [F]irst, the active participation by one individual in the death of another is [by its nature] morally and legally wrong, and second, there is no certainty that abuses can be prevented by anything less than a complete prohibition.
>
> Creating an exception for the terminally ill might therefore frustrate the purpose of the legislation in protecting the vulnerable because adequate guidelines to control abuse are difficult or impossible to develop.

THE LAWS OF OTHER COUNTRIES

Finally, Justice Sopinka considered the laws of other "Western democracies" at that time (1993). Apparently, he did this to determine if there were other laws comparable to the ruling sought by Sue Rodriguez. He said: "Nowhere is assisted suicide expressly permitted, and most countries have provisions expressly dealing with assisted suicide which are at least as restrictive as ours [section 241]."

He noted that the European Commission on Human Rights (a tribunal with many judicial powers over members of the

European Union) had considered the appeal of a decision under the English Suicide Act of 1961, under which a member of a voluntary euthanasia association was charged and convicted of conspiracy to aid suicide by putting people in touch with others who then assisted them. The conviction was appealed on the ground of an invasion of the right to privacy as guaranteed by Article 10 of the European Convention for the Protection of Human Rights and Fundamental Freedoms. The European Commission sustained the conviction.

Yet, Justice Sopinka recognized that there were exceptions, even within Western democracies. He pointed to the Netherlands where, at the time he wrote his opinion, he noted that assisted suicide and voluntary active mercy killing were officially illegal, and no prosecutions were pressed so long as there was compliance with medically established guidelines. He wrote: "Critics of the Dutch approach point to evidence suggesting that [unwilling] involuntary active euthanasia (which is not permitted by the guidelines) is being practised to an increasing degree. This worrisome trend supports the view that a relaxation of the absolute prohibition takes us down the slippery slope."

He further noted that two American states, Washington and California, in 1991 and 1992 respectively, placed on the ballot propositions which would have permitted physician-assisted suicide under specific conditions to ensure voluntary and rational choice. Both propositions were defeated by the same margin — 54 to 46 percent. (As we shall see, such proposals, placed again on the ballot, were approved by voters.)

These were the conclusions reached by Justice Sopinka as to the balance between the interest of the individual and that of the state:

- Canada and other "Western democracies" recognize as a central principle the sanctity of life. Where there are exceptions to that principle, they are limited and narrow. Within such exceptions, the interests of the individual and human dignity are rights protected by the Charter.

- In the dying process, a line has been drawn by society between active and passive involvement by third persons. It is one matter for a patient to order the withdrawal of medical treatment even if this means the patient's death. It is an entirely different matter for a third person to actively initiate the process of death.
- The reason for this line of separation, said Justice Sopinka, goes back centuries in the common law: No one, including a physician, has the right to impose a procedure on another adult without that person's consent. And, when the procedure is one of actively causing the death of another, even consent by the patient will not allow the physician the right to so act.

As noted, the vote of justices in the Rodriguez case was 5–4. The dissenting justices issued three different opinions, two of which (of some length) will be discussed.

THE DISSENT OF JUSTICE MCLACHLIN
Central to the dissent of then Justice McLachlin was the role of section 7 of the Charter. She set out the majority position in relation to section 7. Then, she turned to the Court's decision in *The Queen v. Morgentaler* [1988], 1 *Supreme Court of Canada Reports* 30. There, she said, the provisions of the Criminal Code in relation to limiting therapeutic abortions only to hospitals — and only then when they were approved by hospital committees that did not necessarily follow common guidelines — were found to violate section 7 of the Charter.

To Justice McLachlin, the Morgentaler case offered precedent in the sense that its reasoning should have been followed in the Rodriguez case. She wrote:

It is sufficient for the purposes of this case to note that a legislative scheme which limits the right of a person to deal with her body as she chooses may violate the principles of fundamental justice under section 7 of the Charter if the limit is arbitrary....

This brings us to the critical issue in this case. Does the fact that the [law] which regulates suicide denies to Sue Rodriguez the right to commit suicide because of her physical incapacity hence a violation of section 7? Under the law Parliament has set up, the physically able person is legally allowed to end his or her life; he or she cannot be criminally penalized for attempting or committing suicide.

But the person who is physically unable to accomplish the act is not similarly allowed to end her life. This is the effect of §241 of the Criminal Code which criminalizes the act of assisting a person to commit suicide and which may render the person who desires to commit suicide a conspirator to the crime....

What is the difference between suicide and assisted suicide that justifies making the one lawful and the other a crime, that justifies allowing some this choice, while denying it to others?

The argument is essentially this. There may be no reason on the facts of Sue Rodriguez's case for denying to her the choice to end her life, a choice that those physically able have available to them. Nevertheless, she must be denied that choice because of the danger that other people may wrongfully abuse the power they have over the weak and the ill, and may end the lives of these people persons against their consent.

Thus, Sue Rodriguez is asked to bear the burden of the chance that other people in other situations may act criminally to kill others or improperly sway them to suicide. She is asked to serve as a scapegoat [emphasis added].

The approach taken by the majority opinion, said Justice McLachlin, was wrong. Rather, one must bear in mind the goal of the law: *Does it violate a particular person's interest under section 7 of the Charter?* "The principles of fundamental justice," she said, "require that each person, considered individually, be treated fairly by the law."

THE ROLE OF SECTION 1: BURDEN OF PROOF

Recall that section 1 subjects rights granted under the Charter to reasonable limits prescribed by law as can be demonstrably justified in a free and democratic society. And, once it has been shown that a fundamental right (section 7) has been violated, the burden is on the government to justify the violation.

Justice McLachlin reviewed the reasoning of the majority and found it lacking in terms of meeting the tests of section 1:

- *A cloak for murder?* Justice McLachlin said that the majority justified the law against assisted suicide as a cloak not to prevent suicide, but to prevent murder. It is doubtful, she stated, whether such law should be used to violate fundamental principles of justice. She added that it is not clear that a law against assisted suicide is necessary. She said that there already are laws dealing with murder and degrees of homicide. And, she suggested that if there were a danger that assisted suicide might be linked to involuntary deaths of the aged and disabled, other more proportionate ways may be found to deal with the problem than a total ban on assisted suicide.

• *Passing depression.* Still, isn't it possible that a desire for assisted suicide may spring from depression? And, couldn't such depression be a "passing" matter? Or couldn't it spring from the undue influence of others?

Justice McLachlin said these concerns centre on the question of *consent.* But how could these concerns relate to Sue Rodriguez? She was a person of sound mind who, all members of the Court seemed to acknowledge, was fully aware of the important facts relating to her life and the reality of suicide.

Still, Justice McLachlin said, suppose there were a need to check on consent — to make sure that such consent was with knowledge freely given. There were means for affecting such checks. Here Justice McLachlin cited the dissent of Chief Justice Lamer and, by inference, the dissent of the chief justice of the British Columbia Court of Appeal, noted before:

1. Physician-assisted suicide would be subject to court review under standards set out by the chief justice.
2. Counselling or advising people to commit suicide would remain a crime under section 241(a) of the Criminal Code.
3. There could be prosecution for murder or other forms of homicide.

Justice McLachlin wrote: "The cause of death having been established, it will be for the person who administered the cause to establish that the death was really a suicide to which the deceased consented."

THE DISSENT OF CHIEF JUSTICE LAMER

According to Chief Justice Lamer, section 15 of the Charter was another basis in support of Sue Rodriguez. It provides: "Every individual is equal before and under the law and has the right to equal protection of the law without discrimination and, in particular, without discrimination based on race, national or ethnic origin, colour, religion, sex, age, or mental or physical disability."

Chief Justice Lamer stated: "It is only on account of their physical disability that persons unable to commit suicide unassisted are unequally affected by §241(b) of the Criminal Code.... [Such persons] fall within the classes of persons covered by section 15(1) of the Charter, which contains no definition of the phrase physical disability. Persons whose movement is so limited are even to some degree the classic case of what is meant by a person with a disability in ordinary speech...."

But, are the physically disabled — that is, those seeking assisted suicide — deprived of something that can be called a benefit? The chief justice said: "Without expressing any opinion on the moral value of suicide, I am forced to conclude that the fact that persons unable to end their own lives cannot choose suicide because they do not legally have access to assistance is — in legal terms — a disadvantage [called a benefit under section 15 of the Charter] giving rise to the application of section 15(1) of the Charter...."

SECTION 1 OF THE CHARTER: A DEFENCE?

Under the reasoning of Chief Justice Lamer, a violation of section 15 of the Charter had occurred. He then asked whether there was a defence to a section 15 violation under section 1 of the Charter.

This is how the chief justice answered the question: He said that the legislative purpose of section 241 is the protection of vulnerable persons, whether they are consenting or not, from the intervention of others in decisions about the planning and commission of suicide. Underlying this purpose is the principle of preserving life — a valid purpose. Yet at the same time, he said, Parliament gave to physically able persons the right to choose suicide.

The problem and the fault in terms of finding a valid defence under section 1, the chief justice stated, was in an overly broad section 241. That provision was not framed in terms of the vulnerable. Rather, it covered *all* the physically disabled — including those fully able to decide for themselves as to suicide free from any outside pressure.

He said that Rodriguez, on the record, was one of those disabled but clearly able to make her own rational decision concerning assisted suicide. He wrote:

> Sue Rodriguez is and will remain mentally competent. She has testified at trial to the fact that she alone, in consultation with her physicians, wishes to control the decision-making regarding the timing and circumstances of her death. I see no reason to disbelieve her. Nor has the Crown suggested that she is being wrongfully influenced by anyone.
>
> Ms. Rodriguez has also emphasized that she remains and wishes to remain free not to avail herself of the opportunity to end her own life should that be her eventual choice. *The issue here is whether Parliament is justified in denying her the ability to make this choice lawfully, as could any physically able person* [emphasis added].

THE MAJORITY RESPONDS

Justice Sopinka, for the Court majority, argued that section 1 of the Charter provides a complete defence to any section 15 violation. Indeed, he said, the only point of difference with the chief justice in the Rodriguez case was whether section 241(b) could be drafted in less sweeping terms. For the Court to do so, he said, would create an exception for persons like Rodriguez, and it would limit the flexibility that Parliament ought to have in dealing with "this contentious and morally laden issue." He continued:

> There is no halfway measure that could be relied upon with assurance to fully achieve the legislation's purpose; first because the purpose extends to the protection of the life of the terminally ill.... Part of this purpose, as I have explained ... is to discourage the terminally ill from choosing death over life. Secondly, even if the latter consideration can be stripped from the legislative purpose, we have no assurance that the exception can be made to limit the taking of life to those who are terminally ill and genuinely desire death.

CONTROLS FOR CONSENT: THE CHIEF JUSTICE

Chief Justice Lamer would have declared section 241(b) of the Criminal Code in violation of the Charter. However, he would have allowed time for Parliament to revise the law to meet the concerns of the Court. Also, he would have allowed Sue Rodriguez, and persons in her situation, a remedy. They could choose assisted suicide if they met the following conditions, which in many ways were similar to those the chief justice of the British Columbia Court of Appeal would have set. Meeting such conditions would in the view of Chief Justice Lamer be a constitutional exemption:

- They would have to apply on their own for permission to a superior court.
- Close to the time when they wanted assisted suicide, they would have their treating physician and an

independent psychiatrist certify that the applicant was competent to make a decision to end his or her life, and that the decision was made freely.

- At least one of the signing physicians must be present at the time the applicant commits assisted suicide.
- The physicians must certify that the applicant was or would become physically incapable of committing suicide unassisted, and that they have informed him or her that there is a right to change his or her mind at any time.
- Between the time of court approval and the assisted suicide, one of the certifying physicians must examine the applicant daily to confirm that which earlier was certified in court. Any approved certification would last only for a fixed period of time.
- The act causing death must be that of the applicant, and not of anyone else.

YOU BE THE JUDGE

EASING PAIN, OR HOMICIDE?

The case that follows was suggested in oral argument before the Supreme Court of Canada in the Rodriguez case.

THE FACTS

Sarah H., like Sue Rodriguez, suffers from Lou Gehrig's disease. Like Rodriguez, she is forty-two and married, with a child. She is highly intelligent. She has had a full career as a research scientist. Her physicians estimate that she has about two to eight months to live.

She wants to live her life as fully as possible. To her, this means having the mental alertness to complete her research work and being with her family as a wife and mother. She wants to avoid what she calls mind-numbing medications — even though they are painkillers — until the last possible moment.

Paralysis, which is part of the disease, has accelerated. She is physically inactive, except for slow speech and eye movement. She wants what she has called death with dignity. She wants assistance in dying.

Sarah H. is aware of the Rodriguez case. She has consulted with her physician and requested the following of him:

> On my instructions, I want you to inject into me pain killers. I will do this at a point when it will no longer matter to me if my life continues. You are to continue injecting such pain killers until I feel that the pain, which is quite unbearable, has ended. You have my permission to provide such care, even if it results in death. It is understood that I am not asking you to cause my death. My instructions are intended only to ensure that I have the least amount of pain as possible.

THE ISSUE

If the doctor administers the pain killers as Sarah H. requested, and if she dies as a result, may a charge of unlawfully assisting in the suicide of another in violation of section 241(b) of Criminal Code be laid?

POINTS TO CONSIDER

- Section 241(b) of the Criminal Code makes it an offence to assist another to commit suicide.
- A physician, like any other person, may be charged with an offence under the Criminal Code.
- In the Rodriguez case, a majority of the Supreme Court of Canada upheld section 241(b) from an attack under the Charter.
- A physician has the right to care for his or her patient and, in that regard, subject to the patient's direct instructions to the contrary, to do what is necessary to ease that patient's pain.
- As we shall see, a unanimous Supreme Court of Canada in the Carter case which follows overruled the Rodriguez decision. But, let us assume that the law relating to homicide remains.

DISCUSSION

Whether the doctor would be open to a charge under section 241 of the Criminal Code depends on the answer to this question: What was the intent of the doctor in giving the patient pain killers?

If the doctor's intent was to kill Sarah H., then the doctor could be charged and presumably convicted under section 241 (or the law relating to homicide). If the intent was to ease her pain knowing, at the same time, that the injections would likely speed her death, then the doctor probably could not be convicted under section 241 (or the law relating to homicide).

Justice Sopinka, speaking for the Court majority in the Rodriguez case, said that there could be important problems of proof for the Crown prosecutor. Based on the facts relating to Sarah H., it would not be an easy burden for the Crown to carry in obtaining a conviction against the doctor so long as the doctor did not inject any significantly greater amount of pain killers than other doctors in comparable cases.

In the Rodriguez case, Justice Sopinka stated:

> The fact that doctors may deliver palliative care [to ease pain] to terminally ill patients without fear of sanction [punishment], it is argued, [limits] to an even greater degree any legitimate distinction which can be drawn between assisted suicide and what are currently acceptable forms of medical treatment.
>
> The administration of drugs designed for pain control in dosages which the physician knows will hasten death constitutes active contribution to death by any standard.
>
> However, the distinction drawn here is one based upon intention. In the case of palliative care, the intention is to ease pain, while in the case of assisted suicide, the intention is undeniably to cause death....

> In my view, distinctions based upon intent are important, and in fact form the basis of our criminal law.
>
> While factually the distinction may, at times, be difficult to draw, legally it is clear. The fact that, in some cases, the third party will, under the guise of palliative care, commit euthanasia [mercy killing] or assist in suicide and go unsanctioned due to the difficulty of proof, cannot be said to render the existence of the prohibition fundamentally unjust.

THE DEATH OF SUE RODRIGUEZ

Sue Rodriguez chose the date and place of her death: February 12, 1994, at her home on Vancouver Island, British Columbia. Neither her husband nor her nine year-old son — nor any other family members or friends — were present, although her husband was informed of the date. The only persons who were with her and could describe what occurred were an unnamed physician and an outspoken ally in Rodriguez's attempt to legalize physician-assisted suicide: Svend Robinson, an NDP Member of Parliament.

Following Rodriguez's death, Robinson notified her physician — a palliative care physician who had examined her a few days before and pronounced her as being "comfortable." He also notified the police and called Rodriguez's friends. The physician came to Rodriguez's home, examined her body, and pronounced her dead. She then notified the coroner.

The unnamed physician had left at the point when Rodriguez was dead. The pathologist who conducted an autopsy on February

16 announced that he could not determine the cause of death. The coroner then turned to toxicological examination. The results of that examination determined that Sue Rodriguez had died from consuming a mixture of prescription drugs.

Robinson refused to divulge the method of death. He was quoted as saying: "Sue remained serene and calm throughout, and in total control. She faced her death with incredible courage and dignity. I held her in my arms. She peacefully lapsed into unconsciousness and stopped breathing about two hours later. The [unnamed] doctor then left."

Sgt. Wayne Squire of the Sydney RCMP detachment, investigating the death, said: "Mere presence at the scene of an offence is not enough to support a criminal charge. As long as he [Robinson] didn't take an active role in the death, then we don't see how he can be involved."

Still, Robinson, though asserting that he had not violated the law, retained a prominent Toronto criminal lawyer to act for him if it became necessary. However, no criminal charges were laid by the Crown in the death of Sue Rodriguez.

AN ONGOING CANADIAN DEBATE

On April 21, 2010, the Canadian House of Commons voted on a private member's bill brought by Bloc Québécois MP Francine Lalonde to legalize assisted suicide. While substantial media coverage attended the bill, it failed by a vote of 228 to 59. The vote was open. The parties did not attempt to discipline members to vote for or against.

Steven Fletcher, a Conservative Cabinet minister who was a quadriplegic, abstained in the vote — a position he had announced earlier. He said:

Mr. Speaker, I rise on a point of order. I would like to be recorded as abstaining on this bill. The reason is I believe end of life issues need to be debated more in our country. I believe that life should be the first choice but not the only choice, and that we have to ensure that resources and supports are provided to Canadians so that choice is free.

I believe, when all is said and done, the individual is ultimately responsible. I want to make this decision for myself, and if I cannot, I want my family to make the decision. I believe most Canadians, or many Canadians, feel the same. As William Henley said in his poem *Invictus*: "I am the master of my fate. I am the captain of my soul."

In 2014 Fletcher introduced two private members bills that would have allowed for physician-assisted suicide. The bills failed to be considered by Parliament. But, as we shall see, the issue came before the Supreme Court of Canada, which, in some cases, afforded Charter protection for physician-assisted suicide.

TWO ETHICISTS, TWO POINTS OF VIEW

Two prominent academics set out different views on euthanasia in the *Globe and Mail*. A partial statement of those views are included here only for the purpose of assisting in what might be an ongoing discussion of shaping public policy within the context of the Charter.

The first is that of Margaret Somerville, professor of law and medicine at McGill University. (Her comments were in response to a letter which appeared in the *Globe and Mail*. However, her comments stand by themselves.) The second is that of Arthur Schafer, director of the Centre for Professional and Applied Ethics at the University of Manitoba.

MARGARET SOMERVILLE SPEAKS

Anthony Westell is wrong when he wrote on this page that he has a right to die. In legal theory, that would mean that someone else has a duty to kill him and, even if euthanasia and assisted suicide were legalized, there would be no such obligation. But he certainly can, and arguably may die when he wants to by committing suicide. If we accept that he may do so (that is, the law regards him as having a legal privilege to do so), then the rest of us must not interfere with the exercise of that privilege. That means that treatment must not be imposed if he is brought to a hospital emergency room or paramedics are called because he is in the process of dying by suicide.

Such an approach is contrary to current medical practice. In deciding whether to change that practice, we would consider not only Mr. Westell's claims to exercise his legal privilege, but also the harmful effects that respecting that privilege would have on others. These include health-care professionals who will be forced to stand by and watch him die, and the impact of their doing that on the ethos of medicine as a whole. They also include individuals who attempt suicide as a cry for help, or who want to die at the time but later are grateful they were treated.

Mr. Westell fails to consider these or any other wider implications of his claim. On the contrary, he assumes *no clear public interest is served* by prohibiting euthanasia and assisted suicide. His argument for assisted suicide is based entirely on intense individualism — it's my death and nobody else's business how it occurs, especially not the state's business to interfere with through law....

Mr. Westfell ... argues that the burden of proof should be on those who oppose the civil liberty ... of a civilized death. Until the enactment of the Charter of Rights and Freedoms, the burden of proof was on those wanting to change the law to show that change was justified. But by framing claims that a given law breaches Charter rights and therefore should be changed reverses this burden. Those accused of breaching such rights have the burden of proving they are justified, within the terms of the Charter, in doing so.

This change of the burden of proof matters, because its allocation is not a neutral act. When there is equal doubt as to whether one or the other course of conduct should prevail, the persons with the burden of proof lose their case. Fortunately, a majority of the Supreme Court of Canada ruled in the Sue Rodriguez case that the prohibition on assisted suicide in the Criminal Code did not breach Charter rights.

Mr. Westell clearly does not understand the distinction between legalization and decriminalization. Suicide was decriminalized by Parliament, not legalized. Consequently, his argument that it *can't be illegal to assist in this legal act* is misguided....

Finally, Mr. Westell concludes, as I will, with one important reason that, in stark contrast to him, I see as a powerful reason not to legalize euthanasia or assisted suicide. Once the principle [allowing these interventions] will be established ... why [should] civilized death be available only to the dying (*Globe and Mail*, December 2, 2004)?

ARTHUR SCHAFER SPEAKS

When I began teaching ethics to undergraduate medical students in 1970, the hot-button issues were passive and indirect euthanasia. *Passive euthanasia* referred to withholding or withdrawal of life support, from the motive of mercy, usually at the request of a dying patient. Doctors used to worry about both the ethics and the legality of hastening a patient's death by pulling the plug.

Indirect euthanasia was the term in use to describe the administration of large, sometimes very large, doses of analgesia with the direct aim of relieving pain but in the knowledge that, indirectly, this pain relief was likely to depress the patient's respiratory system and thereby bring on death more quickly.

Passive euthanasia is now called *appropriate care*. Today it is universally practised in Canadian hospitals, and no physician has been charged with a criminal offence for withholding or withdrawing life support, whether at the request of a dying patient, in compliance with a living will, or at the request of the patient's family when the patient was no longer competent....

In 1992, Nancy B., a 25-year-old quadriplegic, told a Quebec Superior Court judge: *I am fed up with living on a respirator. It's no life.* The court ruled in her favour, and she was disconnected from life support. This case helped to establish that, in Canada, a competent adult has the right to refuse life-prolonging treatment.

Indirect euthanasia is now seen as merely a form of palliative care. A physician who denies adequate pain relief to a dying patient because of fears that the analgesic might cause death would be considered unprofessional. Today, many Canadian hospitals have palliative care wards in which the overall treatment goal is to keep the patient comfortable rather than to prolong life. In these wards and in hospices for the dying, there is little hesitation in administering whatever dose of painkiller is required for comfort, even when the foreseeable consequence is hastened death.

One important lesson to be learned from these historical debates is that not all slopes are slippery. Opponents of so-called passive euthanasia balefully predicted that, if doctors were allowed to withhold or withdraw life support, we would immediately find ourselves on a slippery slope. Doctors who pulled the plug on dying patients would become desensitized or even brutalized. Hospitals would become cruel and dehumanized places. Patients would come to think of their doctors as executioners. The fundamental social value of respect for life would be debased. The elderly and the vulnerable would be at high risk of merciless killing.

But experience has shown that what happened was exactly the opposite of what was predicted by the naysayers: Doctors and hospitals have become kinder and gentler, patients' wishes are better respected than previously, and society has come to accept the importance of individual autonomy at the end of life.

Let's consider where the euthanasia debate stands today. When palliative care doesn't provide needed relief from severe and intractable suffering, a growing number of hospitals now offer sedation to unconsciousness: *the patient is rendered terminally unconscious and food and fluids are then discontinued.* For many people, however, terminal sedation seems an undignified way to end one's life. Instead, they seek physician-assisted suicide.

Physician-assisted suicide has been legal in Oregon for 11 years [at the time of writing this comment in 2009] and accounts for about one out of every thousand deaths a year. But, although it's not used often, one in six patients discusses this option with their family, and one in fifty raises it with their doctor. In other words, the safeguards appear to work. Few people opt for physician-assisted suicide, but many take comfort from the knowledge that, if their lives became unbearable, they can request — and be given — assistance to die.

Of course, as doctors sometimes acknowledge, euthanasia and assisted suicide are practised secretly in both the United States and Canada. Where these practices are illegal, they are practised in the dark and thus more likely to result in mistakes and abuse.

Critics widely predicted that legalizing physician-assisted suicide would be a slippery slope to cutbacks in palliative care. Society would reason: Why offer expensive comfort care to suffering patients when it's cheaper to hasten their deaths? In practice, the opposite has occurred. Oregon legislation requires that dying patients be offered a full range of options, and the state has become a leader in palliative and end-of-life care.

Is it too much to hope that our legislators might learn from recent history? When it comes to end-of-life care, Canadians should be able to choose among a full range of options, including first-rate palliative care and physician-assisted suicide. With proper safeguards in place to ensure openness and accountability, there's no reason to deny people the help they want and need (*Globe and Mail*, November 5, 2009).

RODRIGUEZ OVERRULED: THE CARTER CASE

One part of the majority opinion in the Rodriguez decision noted that, at the time, there had been no Canadian, American, British, or European legislative endorsement of the right to die by means of physician-assisted suicide. However, since *Rodriguez*, the topic has remained a subject for discussion and legislative action — as well as court review.

The majority of the Supreme Court of Canada noted that, in effect, one person, namely, Sue Rodriguez, was asking the Court to overturn an established line of important cases. If the Court had acquiesced in the position set out by her, it would have gone further than she requested. The Court would have ruled as to all persons disabled, not just as to Rodriguez, and it was she — and she alone — who sought relief from the Court. This became a point to distinguish the Rodriguez from the Carter case.

It may be argued that once the Supreme Court of Canada has spoken on an issue, that is the end of the matter and the issue cannot be revisited. If the facts are essentially the same, then the first case should govern. In law, this principle, long established, has a name: *stare decisis*.

The primary complainants in the Carter case were two women suffering from terminal illnesses who sought physician-assisted suicide. Both died before the Court rendered its decision.

Can it not be said that the facts of *Rodriguez* and *Carter* were essentially the same? The answer certainly must be "yes" to the extent that they related to specific individuals suffering from the same life-taking illness. But, was the public policy criminalizing physician-assisted suicide the same in the two cases? Indeed, was it the same in terms of what the Supreme Court of Canada referred to as the Western democracies?

It is here that the Supreme Court of Canada drew a line of difference (not the only one, but one to be sure) between *Rodriguez* and *Carter*. Again, bear in mind that the Court in *Carter* spoke as "the Court" — not as individual judge opinions.

The Carter decision was the opinion of all nine justices. It was an opinion circulated among the nine justices and one to which all nine justices individually agreed. This was not an opinion of an individual justice. Nor was it, as in *Rodriguez*, an opinion signed off on by a majority of five against a minority of four justices.

In *Carter*, this was how "the Court" explained the rule of *stare decisis*:

The doctrine that lower courts must follow decisions of higher courts is fundamental to our legal system. It provides certainty while permitting the orderly development of the law in incremental steps. However, *stare decisis* is not a straitjacket that condemns the law to *stasis* [that is, to maintaining a balance].

Trial courts may reconsider settled rulings of higher courts in two situations: (1) where a new legal issue is raised; and (2) where there is a change in the circumstances or evidence that fundamentally shifts the parameters of the debate....

Both conditions were met in this case. The trial judge explained her decision to revisit *Rodriguez* by noting the changes in both the legal framework for section 7 [of the Charter] and the evidence on controlling the risk of abuse associated with assisted suicide.

The Supreme Court of Canada had before it a detailed trial record of the facts and the law. It was that record which the Court (all nine justices) reviewed and found the trial court's findings essentially reasonable on the major issues. What the Court did not allow was a new trial.

The Court turned to the fundamental issues presented under the Charter of Rights and Freedoms, part of the Constitution of Canada and, as such, the supreme law of the land. Included in section 7 is the right to life. This is what the Court said as to how that right impacts death:

We do not agree that the right to life requires an absolute prohibition on assistance in dying, or that individuals cannot "waive" their right to life. This would create a "duty to live," rather than a "right to life," and would call into question the legality of any consent to the withdrawal or refusal of life-sustaining treatment.

The sanctity of life is one of our fundamental societal values. Section 7 [of the Charter] is rooted in a profound respect for the value of human life.

But section 7 also encompasses life, liberty and security of the person during the passage to death. It is for this reason that the sanctity of life "is no longer seen to require that all human life is preserved at all costs" [citing *Rodriguez*, Justice Sopinka]. And it is for this reason that the law has come to recognize that in certain circumstances, an individual's choice about the end of her life is entitled to respect....

In *Carter*, the Supreme Court reviewed the findings of the trial court as well as relevant cases which also had been set out by the trial court. The Supreme Court stated:

We agree with the trial judge. An individual's response to a grievous and irremediable medical condition is a matter critical to their dignity and autonomy. The law allows people in this situation to request palliative sedation, refuse artificial nutrition and hydration, or request the removal of life-sustaining medical equipment, but denies them the right to request a physician's assistance in dying. This interferes with their ability to make decisions concerning their bodily integrity and medical care and thus trenches on liberty. And by leaving people like Ms. Taylor [a party in the

Carter case] to endure intolerable suffering, it impinges on their security of the person.

The trial court did not abandon the Rodriguez case. Rather, the trial judge, based on the facts and the law, placed *Rodriguez* in the context of the case before her, namely, as an individual suffering from ALS and unable to take that last measure for self-help — suicide — without the intervention and assistance of a physician. The Supreme Court stated in *Carter*: "The trial judge, relying on *Rodriguez*, concluded that the object of the prohibition [against physician-assisted suicide] was to protect vulnerable persons from being induced to commit suicide at a time of weakness."

In one sense, it can be said that the Supreme Court of Canada jettisoned *Rodriguez*. In another sense, however, it can be said that the Court interpreted *Rodriguez* to accommodate the object of the law, namely, protection of the vulnerable. Put differently perhaps, the Court stated:

> The question is not whether Parliament has chosen the least restrictive means, but whether the chosen means infringe life, liberty or security of the person in a way that has no connection with the mischief contemplated by the legislature. The focus is not broad social impacts, but on the impact of the measure on the individuals whose life, liberty or security of the person is trammelled.
>
> Applying this approach, we conclude that the prohibition on assisted dying is overbroad. The object of the law, as discussed, is to protect vulnerable persons from being induced to commit suicide at a moment of weakness. Canada conceded at trial that the law catches people outside this class.

[Counsel for Canada stated] "It is recognized that not every person who wishes to commit suicide is vulnerable, and that there may be people with disabilities who have a considered, rational and persistent wish to end their own lives." The trial judge accepted that Ms. Taylor was such a person — competent, fully-informed, and free from coercion or duress. It follows that the limitation on their rights is in at least some cases not connected to the objective of protecting vulnerable persons. The blanket prohibition sweeps conduct into its ambit that is unrelated to the law's objective.

REMEDY: COURT AND PARLIAMENT

Based on the facts and the law, the Supreme Court of Canada found that prohibiting physician-assisted suicide within the meaning of the Criminal Code (section 241(b) and section 14) did infringe the section 7 Charter rights of Gloria Taylor (who had died) in a "manner not in accordance with the principles of fundamental justice, and that the infringement is not justified under section 1 of the Charter." The Court continued:

To the extent that the impugned laws deny the section 7 rights of people like Ms. Taylor they are void by operation of section 52 of the Constitution.... It is for Parliament and the provincial legislatures to respond, should they so choose, by enacting legislation consistent with the constitutional parameters set out in these reasons.

The appropriate remedy is therefore a declaration that section 241(b) and section 14 of the Criminal Code are void insofar as they prohibit physician-assisted death for a competent adult person who (1) clearly consents to the termination of life, and (2) has a grievous and irremediable medical condition (including a illness, disease or disability) that causes enduring suffering that is intolerable to the individual in the circumstances of his or her condition. "Irremediable," it should be added, does not require the patient to undertake treatments that are not acceptable to the individual. The scope of this declaration is intended to respond to the factual circumstances of this case. We make no pronouncement on other situations where physician-assisted dying may be sought.

The declaration was suspended for twelve months from the date of the decision. In that time, Parliament and/or the provincial legislatures would be able to enact laws and/or regulations as to physician-assisted dying that fit within the guidelines set by the Court.

BILL 52: SIMILAR TO THE CARTER RULINGS?

In 2014 the National Assembly of Quebec became the first province to legalize doctor-assisted death as part of comprehensive end-of-life legislation. The Quebec act, titled Bill 52, had the support of 80 percent of the MNAs (the Quebec legislators). Quebec Premier Philippe Couillard (Liberal), whose party formed the government of Quebec, allowed his caucus to vote their conscience rather than being held to party policy. The twenty-two MNAs who voted against Bill 52 were all members of the ruling party, including ten Cabinet ministers.

The Quebec law, itself, had been proposed by the Parti Québécois, which had formed the previous government of the province. Parti Québécois MNA Véronique Hivon, who had put forward that bill, said the newly enacted law should not be seen as "medical aid to die" but "end-of-life care."

This is what Bill 52 provides:

- It applies to terminally ill adult patients.
- They must have an incurable illness.
- They must be in an advanced state of irreversible decline in capacities.
- They must be in constant and unbearable physical and psychological pain that doctors believe impossible to relieve through medication.
- The patient request for end-of-life procedure must be supervised by the attending physician and approved through consultation with the hospital's medical team.
- At any time the patient may withdraw a signed request for medical aid in dying.

A GOOD AGE TO DIE?

Dr. Ezekiel Emanuel, a renowned American oncologist (cancer specialist), has said that, in his view, seventy-five is a "good age to die." In 2014 Dr. Emanuel held the Chair at the University of Pennsylvania in medical bioethics and health policy.

Why seventy-five? Dr. Emanuel said: "A good life is not just about stacking up the years and living as long as possible. People need to focus on the quality of life. Setting an actual date for a good time to die helps you focus on what is important in your life."

Dr. Emanuel, fifty-seven when he said this, apparently is in good health. He has no terminal illness and he has no plans to commit suicide. He opposes physician-assisted suicide. Rather, he proposes to simply let nature take its course. When he reaches seventy-five, he will refuse all medical tests and treatments, including the blood pressure medication that he now takes.

In 2010 a Dutch citizens' initiative — "Out of Free Will" — demanded that professional help be allowed to those over the age of seventy in ending their lives if they simply felt tired of living. Those supporting the proposal included former ministers, legal scholars, artists, and physicians.

Who might be included in this group? The *Daily Mail* reported: "They might include widows and widowers overwhelmed by grief, those unwilling to face the frailties of extreme old age, or people determined to 'get out while they're ahead' and meet death on their own terms. The assistants who administered the deadly cocktail of sedatives would need to be certified, campaigners said."

Under current Dutch law, euthanasia by doctors is only legal in cases of "hopeless and unbearable" suffering.

LAW WITHOUT END?

Suppose physician-assisted suicide is legalized, having been approved by the Supreme Court of Canada and the Parliament. What impact might that have on the legal liability of physicians?

Physicians assisting another to commit suicide may still find themselves subject to legal liability from disgruntled relatives of the deceased. Physicians, at least under the terms of the Quebec legislation, must operate under that law. For example, there must be medical findings of unbearable pain by the patient seeking to end her/his life. This fact must be proved by the attending physician. Such proof may have to be made at trial — not always an easy task (both emotionally and as a matter of costs).

PUBLIC OPINION

Since *Rodriguez*, polls have been taken to determine public opinion concerning physician-assisted suicide. The Angus Reid

Institute announced in November 2014 the results of its then new poll of 1,504 Canadians. It stated that Canadians "overwhelmingly support physician-assisted suicide. Indeed, a hard core of such support — so-called 'enthusiasts' — support physician-assisted suicide even in cases that do not involve pain or imminent death, but simply a wish to die."

The *National Post*, referring to pollsters, stated: "These enthusiasts, making up a solid 37% of the population, are very supportive of the right to die across a wide range of scenarios, from a sense of meaninglessness or being a burden to one's family or even being an inmate on a life sentence who wishes to end it all early, all the way to late stage terminal disease with intense pain (*National Post*, December 16, 2014)."

A SLIPPERY SLOPE?

There was no individual opinion in the Carter case. As noted, the decision was signed as the opinion of "the Court." This gave the ruling added weight. It was an "institutional" decision. Questions remain as to how the decision will be implemented by Parliament and the provinces.

But, this does not mean that the decision uniformly is accepted — especially as to what the future might bring. What are the limits to legislative and/or court action? Is it possible for the ruling in the Carter case to be extended to euthanasia as applied to children or the mentally incompetent?

Andrew Coyne wrote:

> What can one say about a ruling that finds a right to death in a section of the constitution devoted to the right to life — that does so in breezy defiance, not just of Parliament's stated preferences, but of the Court's own ruling in a similar case, rendered

two decades before? The Court goes to elaborate and unconvincing lengths to suggest it had been moved by changes in "the matrix of legislative and social facts" since then. The reality, one suspects, is rather simpler. It did it because it wanted to (*National Post*, February 13, 2015).

In 2014 the Belgian King signed into law a bill enacted by that nation's Parliament that allows a critically ill child as young as twelve to be put to death by his/her doctor with the consent of a psychiatrist or psychologist who certifies that the child is conscious and aware of what is being done. This law is similar to one enacted in the Netherlands. Both were approved by large majorities of their respective legislatures.

EDITORIAL COMMENT

The *Globe and Mail* made the following editorial comment on *Carter v. Canada (Attorney General)*:

> "It is a crime in Canada to assist another person in ending her own life." Those are the opening lines of the Supreme Court's unanimous decision striking down that very section of the Criminal Code. "People who are grievously and irremediably ill," write the judges, "cannot seek a physician's assistance in dying and may be condemned to a life of severe and intolerable suffering. A person facing this prospect has two options: She can take her own life prematurely, often by violent or dangerous means, or can suffer until death comes from natural causes. The choice is cruel."
>
> The Supreme Court's remedy for this cruel

choice comes down on the right side of justice. The judges have given Parliament a year to rewrite the Criminal Code to permit willing physicians to assist those who wish to end their lives, but only under a narrow set of circumstances. And the principles it has laid out for crafting a new law are sound. In fact, they read like the terms of Quebec's physician-assisted suicide law, Canada's first.

The law was passed last year with widespread support, including from this newspaper, but it ran smack into a legal wall: It permitted what criminal law forbade. On Friday, the Supreme Court resolved that legal conflict by ordering a rewrite of the Criminal Code.

The Supreme Court says that the old ban on physician-assisted suicide was too broad. In cases where the person in question is an adult of sound mind and clearly wishes to end their life, and where that person is suffering from a severe and incurable medical condition that causes intolerable suffering, the court says that the law must no longer forbid a physician from assisting in ending their life.

But the court is also careful to say that its ruling should not be read as obliging doctors to assist a suicide, even under the conditions of clear consent, incurable illness and intolerable suffering. The Charter [of Rights and Freedoms] is a careful balancing act of rights and obligations, and doctors have rights too, notably rights of freedom of religion and conscience.

When Parliament rewrites the law, it should empower willing physicians to offer this treatment to appropriate patients. It must not, however, force any physician to do so. The Supreme Court has struck the right balance (*Globe and Mail,* February 6, 2015).

SHAPING A NEW LAW

Note what the Supreme Court of Canada did not order: It did not require any governmental authority to rewrite the law, either criminal or civil. It simply suspended the coming into effect of its order for one year from the date of its decision.

In that time the government of Canada could, if it so desired, study and consider what steps, if any, it might take to regulate physician-assisted suicide.

Or the government could do nothing. The result of doing nothing, among other things, would be that the criminal law provision, as it had stood, would be of no force and effect. This could result in the provinces — outside the criminal law — drafting regulations for physician-assisted suicide in the context of safe medical practice.

Dr. Chris Simpson, president of the Canadian Medical Association, stated that Canadian doctors want a "seat at the [drafting] table to ensure legislation is drafted in a way that protects vulnerable people (*Toronto Star,* February 6, 2015)."

André Picard wrote:

> Civil libertarians are suggesting that no laws are required to regulate the provision of physician-assisted death. Rather, it should be an individual decision made between the patient and the physician, like any other medical procedure.
>
> Others believe that more formal rules are required to avoid abuses — like hastened death being imposed on the frail elderly, people with

profound disabilities, and those with severe mental illnesses. (All of which would be made unethical, it should be made clear.) (*Globe and Mail*, February 6, 2015.)

AN EARLY RESPONSE FROM DOCTORS

Sheryl Ubelacker, in *Canadian Press*, provided an early response from Canadian doctors to the Court's decision. She set out some of the questions being asked by medical organizations and the answers provided:

Question: What do doctors now (February 2015) tell suffering patients who ask them for help to die?

Answer: The Canadian Medical Association (CMA) is advising its 80,000 members that the law prohibiting medically assisted death is in effect for a year, giving government time to revamp the legislation. "So nothing changes over the next year while the details are being sorted out," said CMA president Dr. Chris Simpson.

"In general, we want the process to be pretty extraordinarily robust and careful with a lot of steps," said Simpson, including safeguards to protect the vulnerable and to ensure the person seeking to end their life isn't being influenced or coerced by others, even subtly.

"So I would envision multiple steps with more than one doctor, maybe even a panel or some sort of a board that evaluates all of the complexities of this. Because ultimately, at the individual patient level ... it's not an emergency that needs to be done right away. There's time for a process to be thoughtful and ensure that only the people who truly should have medical aid in dying get it."

Question: What about a patient who is physically incapable of giving themselves a fatal drug dose — because of quadriplegia or advanced ALS, for instance?

Answer: Simpson calls this one of the "important nitty-gritty details" yet to be worked out. It's a question that needs to be explored by doctors groups, legislators and legal experts as a framework for how medical aid in dying will actually be delivered.

"A lot of doctors regard the prescribing of a lethal substance as the moral equivalent to actually administering a lethal substance," he said. And while hooking up an IV and giving a fatal dose could be done by any trained physician, "many doctors are saying there should be another class of clinicians who does only this."

"I'm not sure that really absolves anybody because the hard work is in the decision-making. The hard work is not in hooking up the IV."

Question: The Supreme Court ruling says Canadians who are enduring intolerable physical or mental suffering have the right to seek medical help to end their lives. But what constitutes mental suffering and where would the line be drawn?

Answer: Padraic Carr, president of the Canadian Psychiatric Association (CPA), said that's one area of the judgment, in particular, that needs further legal clarification:

"Every patient is different and it's unclear who would meet that legal test or what they define as intolerable, enduring suffering," he said of the nine justices' unanimous decision.

Carr said their ruling speaks to four points in which physician-assisted death may be considered: where a patient is competent; clearly consents; has what they define as a grievous and irremediable condition; and has enduring intolerable suffering.

"I think it would be very difficult for a patient who has a severe mental illness to meet these four criteria."

Question: People with clinical depression and certain other psychiatric disorders are often suicidal. How would doctors tease out whether a patient's desire to die is a result of their illness and might be alleviated with treatment?

Answer: Carr said the court ruled that a patient must be "competent" to obtain medically assisted death, a term which psychiatrists call the "capacity to make decisions."

Capacity means a patient must: be able to make a choice; have the ability to understand the relevant information around that choice; must appreciate their situation and the consequence of making the choice; and demonstrate that they can manipulate that information rationally, he said.

"So depression and other psychiatric illnesses,

including psychotic disorders, can certainly influence your insight and judgment and they can also affect that ability to appreciate your situation and to manipulate that information rationally. So all of those would be included in any capacity assessment."

While the 4,700-member CPA has no official position on the court's ruling as yet, Carr said he can't imagine a scenario in which a patient would meet all those criteria and their situation be thought hopeless.

"It would be a rare instance in psychiatry where a condition would be considered irremediable. Even when someone is called clinically resistant, there are still other treatments that may work" (*Canadian Press*, February 13, 2015).

SWITZERLAND: "SUICIDE TOURISM"?

In the Carter case, the Supreme Court of Canada specifically noted the role of a Swiss "suicide clinic." Swiss law has permitted assisted suicide since 1942. The law does not require a physician to be present, and it does not require the recipient to be a resident of the country. What the law does forbid is "inciting and assisting suicide ... for selfish motives." This would appear to include "personal gain."

Lethal drugs may be prescribed as long as the recipient takes an active role in the drug administration. While a mentally-ill person may claim the right to assisted suicide, consent may require examination and approval by a psychiatrist.

A study published in *The Journal of Medical Ethics* in 2014 looked at assisted suicides in Zurich, where Dignitas, the most prominent right-to-die organization, is based. The researchers found that 611 people from thirty-one countries had committed assisted suicide from 2008 to 2012. Since 2009 the number of those arriving from other countries for help with suicide each year has increased steadily. Nearly half of all cases involved people with neurological disorders such as Parkinson's disease and multiple sclerosis — diagnoses that are generally not terminal. Nearly 60 percent of the 611 were women.

All forms of active euthanasia, such as administering lethal injections, remain prohibited in Switzerland. Swiss law only allows providing the means to commit suicide.

REFERENCES AND FURTHER READING

* Cited by the Supreme Court of Canada.

Belluck, Pam. "Switzerland: More Foreigners Drawn by Assisted Suicide, Study Shows." *New York Times*, August 21, 2014.

Branswell, Helen. "Canadian Doctors, Many Hesitant About Assisted Death, Want Role in Legislation." *Toronto Star*, February 6, 2015.

Brean, Joseph. "Not a Controversial Issue in Canada Anymore, Majority Support Assisted Suicide, Poll Finds." *National Post*, December 16, 2014.

Colvin, Eric. "Section Seven of the Canadian Charter of Rights and Freedoms." *Canadian Bar Review* 68 (1989): 560.*

Coyne, Andrew. "Supreme Court Euthanasia Ruling Marks the Death of Judicial Restraint." *National Post*, February 13, 2015.

Dworkin, Robert. *Life's Dominion: An Argument About Abortion, Euthanasia, and Individual Freedom*. New York: Knopf Publishers, 1993.*

Euthanasia, Aiding Suicide and Cessation of Treatment. Law

Reform Commission of Canada, Working Papers 20, 28. Ottawa: Minister of Supply and Services Canada, 1982, 1983.*

McLuhan, Sabina. "How Did Sue Rodriguez Die?" *The Interim*, March 27, 1994.

Norwood, Frances. *The Maintenance of Life: Preventing Social Death through Euthanasia Talk and End-of-Life Care — Lessons from the Netherlands*. Durham, NC: Carolina Academic Press, 2009.

"Offering a Choice to the Terminally Ill." *New York Times*, March 15, 2015.

Otlowski, Margaret. "Mercy Killing Cases in the Australian Criminal Justice System. *Criminal Law Journal* 17 (1993):10.*

Penrose, Mary Margaret. "Assisted Suicide: A Tough Pill to Swallow." *Pepperdine Law Review* 20 (1993): 689.*

Picard, André. "Next Step in Assisted Suicide: Ensuring It Can Be Done Humanely." *Globe and Mail*, February 6, 2015.

"Renowned Doctor Ezekial Emanuel Says 75 Is a Good Age to Die." CBC.ca, December 7, 2014.

Schafer, Arthur. "The Great Canadian Euthanasia Debate." *Globe and Mail*, November 5, 2009.

Schneider, Keith. "Dr. Jack Kevorkian Dies at 83; Backed Assisted Suicide." *New York Times,* June 3, 2011.

Séguin, Rhéal. "Quebec First Province to Adopt Right-to-Die Legislation." *Globe and Mail*, October 12, 2014.

Somerville, Margaret. "It's Not My Right to Die When I Want To." *Globe and Mail,* December 2, 2004.

"The Supreme Court Gets It Right on Assisted Suicide." *Globe and Mail*, February 6, 2015.

Ubelacker, Sheryl. "What Are The Rules Of Assisted Death In Canada? Doctors Respond." *Canadian Press*, February 13, 2015.

5

CHAPTER 5

END OF LIFE

The Carter and Rodriguez cases are important decisions in understanding the role and impact of the Charter of Rights and Freedoms on Canadian society.

In this final chapter our focus is on the limits of the Court's decision in *Carter* and the power and responsibility of the citizenry, especially through provincial and local governments as well as public-interest organizations (such as hospitals and hospices) and the courts, in the context of Court's ruling. Recall that the issue before the courts centred on the right/obligation of physicians to assist their patients in dying.

The patients involved in *Carter* were two women suffering "irremediable" (hopeless) diseases. They were either helpless or close to being helpless, and they were in pain. They wanted a physician's help to end their lives. Some would say they wanted what is called palliative care (comfort). Others might say they simply wanted to end their lives at a point where life was no longer livable.

The Criminal Code, an instrument over which the federal government under the Constitution has authority, declares that no one, including physicians, may assist another to commit suicide. Palliative care — giving patients drugs to ease their pain, even though such drugs might hasten death — could be seen as falling outside these criminal law sections. Health care, however, lies within the authority of the provinces.

Among the questions raised in this chapter are:

- What is palliative care?
- Is palliative care an alternative to physician-assisted death?
- May patients compel doctors to offer assisted suicide?
- Are there means under the Charter for a legislature to enact laws that override a Supreme Court of Canada decision?

DEFINITION OF PALLIATIVE CARE

The following is a description of palliative care set out by the World Health Organization (WHO), a specialized agency within the United Nations concerned with international public health:

> Palliative care is an approach that improves the quality of life of patients and their families facing the problems associated with life-threatening illness, through the prevention and relief of suffering by means of early identification and impeccable assessment and treatment of pain and other problems, physical, psychosocial and spiritual. Palliative care:
>
> - provides relief from pain and other distressing symptoms;
> - affirms life and regards dying as a normal process;

- intends neither to hasten or postpone death;
- integrates the psychological and spiritual aspects of patient care;
- offers a support system to help patients live as actively as possible until death;
- offers a support system to help the family cope during the patient's illness and in their own bereavement;
- uses a team approach to address the needs of patients and their families, including bereavement counselling, if indicated;
- will enhance quality of life, and may also positively influence the course of illness;
- is applicable early in the course of illness, in conjunction with other therapies that are intended to prolong life, such as chemotherapy or radiation therapy, and includes those investigations needed to better understand and manage distressing clinical complications.

Palliative care for children represents a special, albeit closely related field to adult palliative care. WHO's definition of palliative care appropriate for children and their families is as follows:

- Palliative care for children is the active total care of the child's body, mind and spirit, and also involves giving support to the family.
- It begins when illness is diagnosed, and continues regardless of whether or not a child receives treatment directed at the disease.
- Health providers must evaluate and alleviate a child's physical, psychological, and social distress.
- Effective palliative care requires a broad multidisciplinary approach that includes the family and makes

use of available community resources; it can be successfully implemented even if resources are limited.

- It can be provided in tertiary care facilities, in community health centres and even in children's homes.

A DOCTOR'S DUTY

Medical doctors have a special responsibility to their patients and to the province under which they are licensed. While the Hippocratic Oath, dating back centuries, is no longer recited by graduating doctors in most jurisdictions, a general oath, having the central point that they will do no harm to their patients, often is taken. The obligation of medical doctors is to use their skills to help their patients, whether in hospitals, in clinics, or in their own private practices.

We have seen issues that have conflicted doctors and their patients. Sometimes these issues rise to the level of life/death choices. For example, parents and/or their children who, for personal reasons, will not take vaccines thus endanger not just themselves but the community at large. And families, faced with the death of a loved one whom doctors believe is beyond saving, will not allow the machines that enable breathing and life to be disconnected although the medical staff want to allow that patient to die.

In past chapters we have seen how the courts and individuals have drawn lines that shape decisions. In this final chapter, we look at how the medical profession in Canada sees its role, the role of patients, and the role of the state in coming to decisions as to life and death. In a real sense, the role of the doctor in relation to patients is both tested and defined in this human drama.

Often, but not always, the law has vested physicians and/or hospitals with the right to set procedures that can impact end-of-life patient decisions. Here we speak of physician wants and objections voiced individually and through their professional associations, such as the Canadian Medical Association.

This book has centred on the role of the courts — and especially the Supreme Court of Canada — in deciding the legality of laws and actions, especially in terms of how they square with the Charter of Rights and Freedoms, part of the Constitution of Canada and, as such, the highest law of the land.

We note that there are, of course, means under the Charter for a legislature — for Parliament, by way of example (section 33 of the Charter) — to enact laws that override a Supreme Court of Canada decision, such as that in the Carter case. But, even here, there are practical and legal restraints on the exercise of such override powers.

Section 33 of the Charter states:

(1) Parliament or the legislature of a province may expressly declare in an Act of Parliament or of the legislature, as the case may be, that the Act or a provision thereof shall operate notwithstanding a provision included in section 2 or sections 7 to 15.

(2) An Act or a provision of an Act in respect of which a declaration made under this section is in effect shall have such operation as it would have but for the provision of this Charter referred to in the declaration.

(3) A declaration made under subsection (1) shall cease to have effect five years after it comes into force or on such earlier date as may be specified in the declaration.

(4) Parliament or the legislature of a province may re-enact a declaration made under subsection (1).

(5) Subsection (3) applies in respect of a re-enactment made under subsection (4).

It is, for example, possible for Parliament under section 33 of the Charter to override the Supreme Court's Carter decision. But there are time limits on such override decisions. And, perhaps most importantly, there is this practical question: The government of the day must ask itself whether the political costs of such an override are worth the political price. This is especially so, bearing in mind the fact that the Carter decision was one handed down by the full Court, not individuated opinions of single justices. It is, in effect, an institutional decision of those elders vested by law and the Constitution with authority to judge and decide such issues.

But what was it that the Supreme Court decided in *Carter* and, it may be asked, what is our role as citizens in giving further shape to the Court's rulings (including overriding such judgments)?

YOU BE THE JUDGE

RELIGION/ETHICS AND LEGAL DUTIES

THE FACTS

The law examined by the Supreme Court of Canada in the Carter case was one about physician-assisted death. The Court ruled that two challenged provisions under that law were void to the extent they conflicted with the Charter.

The two initial complainants whose lives were ending as a result of illness passed away before the case was decided. There were a number of institutional interveners allowed to make submissions to the Court. Among the interveners was the Canadian Medical Association (the CMA), a professional association with powers that include disciplining of physician members that could result in suspension or revocation of the license to practise medicine.

For purposes of this hypothet, we will assume that three Canadian medical practitioners who spend a considerable amount of time practising in the emergency rooms of hospitals in the cities where they live have concerns about the effect of the Carter decision on their medical practice. All of the three doctors have either religious or ethical concerns about their obligations in relation to the decision.

THE ISSUE

Does the Carter decision impose a legal obligation on doctors to make assisted death available if such action violates their religious and/or their ethical beliefs? This was a point raised by a number of interveners in the Carter case and noted by the Supreme Court of Canada.

POINTS TO CONSIDER

- The concerns of the doctors are real.
- If they were required to assist patients to die, they would have to refuse such orders on personal grounds.
- As a practical matter, it would be difficult for the hospitals where the doctors practise to find replacements for them.

DISCUSSION

In the Carter decision, the Supreme Court addressed this question. The Court stated:

A number of the interveners asked the Court to account for physicians' freedom of conscience and religion when crafting the remedy in this case. The Catholic Civil Rights League, the Faith and Freedom Alliance, the Protection of Conscience Project and the Catholic Health Alliance of Canada all expressed concern that physicians who object to medical assistance in dying on moral grounds may be obligated, based on a duty to act in their patients' best interests, to participate in physician-assisted dying. They ask us to confirm that physicians and other health-care workers cannot be compelled to provide medical aid in dying. They would have the Court direct the legislature to provide robust protection for those who decline to support or participate in physician-assisted dying for reasons of conscience or religion.

The Canadian Medical Association reports that its membership is divided on the issue of assisted suicide. The Association's current policy states that it supports the right of all physicians, within the bounds of the law, to follow their conscience in deciding whether or not to provide aid in dying. It seeks to see that policy reflected in any legislative scheme that may be put forward.

While acknowledging that the Court cannot itself set out a comprehensive regime, the Association asks us to indicate that any legislative scheme must legally protect both those physicians who choose to provide this new intervention to their patients, along with those who do not.

In our view, nothing in the declaration of invalidity which we propose to issue would compel physicians to provide assistance in dying. The declaration simply renders the criminal prohibition invalid.

What follows is in the hands of the physicians' colleges, Parliament, and the provincial legislatures. However, we note — as did Beetz J. in addressing the topic of physician participation in abortion in *R. v. Morgentaler* — that a physician's decision to participate in assisted dying is a matter of conscience and, in some cases, of religious belief....

In making this observation, we do not wish to pre-empt the legislative and regulatory response to this judgment. Rather, we underline that the Charter rights of patients and physicians will need to be reconciled.

A MATTER OF EXEMPTION?

Suppose a hospital is owned and operated by a religious institution. It is clear that the hospital functions under a code of religious beliefs and ethical standards common throughout all of the institution's many hospitals in Canada and, indeed, much of the world.

What the Supreme Court of Canada said in *Carter* applies to all of the organization's hospitals in Canada. A problem has arisen in some of the religious institution's hospitals. These hospitals want an "exemption." They want the right to turn patients in a terminal condition away — to deny them hospital admission if they insist on a right to physician-assisted death within the meaning of the Carter decision.

In effect, such prospective patients would be required to sign a waiver giving up any right to physician-assisted death. Full disclosure to the patients and/or their families would be given as to the nature of the waiver.

How would a court decide the question?

Listen again to what the Court said in *Carter*. It defined its role narrowly in relation to the case it decided. There were provisions of the Criminal Code before it for interpretation. And, the Court ruled that those provisions were in violation of the Charter.

What followed from the Court's decision is in the hands of the physicians' colleges, Parliament, and the provincial legislatures to implement. And, this they must do while also reconciling patient rights with the Charter.

It would seem from the Court's language that if a question arose in terms of how that reconciliation has been effected, the matter may be presented to a court for determination.

The Court declared the two questioned provisions of the Criminal Code invalid. But it suspended this declaration of invalidity for twelve months. The Court stated:

We would issue the following declaration, which is suspended for 12 months.... Section 241(b) and section 14 of the Criminal Code unjustifiably infringe section 7 of the Charter and are of no force or effect to the extent that they prohibit physician-assisted death for a competent adult person who (1) clearly consents to the termination of life and (2) has a grievous and irremediable medical condition (including an illness, disease or disability) that causes enduring suffering that is intolerable to the individual in the circumstances of his or her condition.

We have concluded that the laws prohibiting a physician's assistance in terminating life (Criminal Code, section 241(b) and section 14) infringe Ms. Taylor's section 7 rights to life, liberty and security of the person in a manner that is not in accordance with the principles of fundamental justice, and that the infringement is not justified under section 1 of the Charter.

To the extent that the impugned laws deny the section 7 rights of people like Ms. Taylor they are void by operation of section 52 of the Constitution Act, 1982. It is for Parliament and the provincial legislatures to respond, should they so choose, by enacting legislation consistent with the constitutional parameters set out in these reasons.

WHY THE DELAY? WHAT THE COST?

Usually, there is no easy path to accessing the Supreme Court of Canada. It is not unusual for a matter to take as long as five years to reach the Court. Bear in mind that the Carter case began in 2009 and in one sense ended with the Supreme Court of Canada's decision in 2015 with a declaration of suspension for twelve months.

While the Carter case was "special" in the sense that it presented new and important issues for the Supreme Court of Canada and the numerous institutional interveners in the case, the following data from the Supreme Court of Canada statistics (2004–14 tables) should be noted:

- Application for hearing to the Supreme Court: from a minimum of 4.1 months to a maximum of 7.1 months.
- Decision by the Supreme Court allowing a hearing: from a minimum of 7.7 months to a maximum of 9.4 months.
- Decision of the Supreme Court: from a minimum of 3.7 months to a maximum of 4.4 months.

Ordinarily, costs are an important factor to litigants especially in matters reflecting public policy. The burden imposed, for example, on the British Columbia Civil Rights Association was heavy from the start to the end in the sense of the decision of the Supreme Court of Canada opinion discussed in chapter 4. Precedent seemed to weigh against those who brought the case for remedy to win an award for costs.

In *Carter*, the Supreme Court of Canada seemed to break with tradition. It awarded full legal costs to those who both brought the litigation to trial and appeal. In part, this is what the Court stated in an extensive consideration of the cost question:

> The appellants ask for special costs on a full indemnity basis to cover the entire expense of bringing this case before the courts.
>
> The trial judge awarded the appellants special costs exceeding $1,000,000 on the ground that this

was justified by the public interest in resolving the legal issues raised by the case.... [T]he trial judge relied on *Victoria (City) v. Adams*, 2009 BCCA 563, 100 B.C.L.R. (4th) 28, at para. 188, which set out four factors for determining whether to award special costs to a successful public interest litigant: (1) the case concerns matters of public importance that transcend the immediate interests of the parties, and which have not been previously resolved; (2) the plaintiffs have no personal, proprietary or pecuniary interest in the litigation that would justify the proceeding on economic grounds; (3) the unsuccessful parties have a superior capacity to bear the cost of the proceedings; and (4) the plaintiffs did not conduct the litigation in a abusive, vexatious or frivolous manner. The trial judge found that all four criteria were met in this case.

The Court of Appeal saw no error in the trial judge's reasoning on special costs, given her judgment on the merits. However, as the majority overturned the trial judge's decision on the merits, it varied her costs order accordingly. The majority ordered each party to bear its own costs.

The appellants argue that special costs, while exceptional, are appropriate in a case such as this, where the litigation raises a constitutional issue of high public interest, is beyond the plaintiffs' means, and was not conducted in an abusive or vexatious manner. Without such awards, they argue, plaintiffs will not be able to bring vital issues of importance to all Canadians before the courts, to the detriment of justice and other affected Canadians.

Against this, we must weigh the caution that "[c]ourts should not seek on their own to bring an alternative and extensive legal aid system into being:" *Little Sisters Book and Art Emporium v. Canada (Commissioner of Customs and Revenue)*, 2007 SCC 2, [2007] 1 S.C.R. 38, at para. 44. With this concern in mind, we are of the view that *Adams* sets the threshold for an award of special costs too low. This Court has previously emphasized that special costs are only available in "exceptional" circumstances: *Finney v. Barreau du Québec*, 2004 SCC 36, [2004] 2 S.C.R. 17, at para. 48. The test set out in *Adams* would permit an award of special costs in cases that do not fit that description. Almost all constitutional litigation concerns "matters of public importance." Further, the criterion that asks whether the unsuccessful party has a superior capacity to bear the cost of the proceedings will always favour an award against the government. Without more, special costs awards may become routine in public interest litigation....

In our view, with appropriate modifications, this test serves as a useful guide to the exercise of a judge's discretion on a motion for special costs in a case involving public interest litigants. First, the case must involve matters of public interest that are truly exceptional. It is not enough that the issues raised have not previously been resolved or that they transcend the individual interests of the successful litigant: they must also have a significant and widespread societal impact. Second, in addition to showing that they have no personal, proprietary or pecuniary interest in the litigation that would justify the proceedings on economic grounds, the plaintiffs must show that it would not have been possible to effectively pursue the litigation in question with private funding. In those rare cases, it will be contrary to the interests of justice to ask the individual litigants (or, more likely, pro bono counsel) to bear the majority of the financial burden associated with pursuing the claim.

Where these criteria are met, a court will have the discretion to depart from the usual rule on costs and award special costs.

Finally, we note that an award of special costs does not give the successful litigant the right to burden the defendant with any and all expenses accrued during the course of the litigation. As costs awards are meant to "encourage the reasonable and efficient conduct of litigation" (*Okanagan Indian Band*, at para. 41), only those costs that are shown to be reasonable and prudent will be covered by the award.

Having regard to these criteria, we are not persuaded the trial judge erred in awarding special costs to the appellants in the truly exceptional circumstances of this case. We would order the same with respect to the proceedings in this Court and in the Court of Appeal.

The Carter decision was handed down by the Supreme Court of Canada on February 6, 2015. A month later, André Picard, a *Globe and Mail* columnist, wrote: "The notion that parliamentarians need more than the 12 months granted them by the Supreme Court of Canada to draft a new law on physician-assisted death beggars belief. Legislators have one job: to make laws. They should get to it without delay."

In Picard's view, there had been delay:

1. The prime minister hinted that he might invoke the not-withstanding clause of the Charter (section 33, discussed above). But, he then "backed away from that position."
2. The parliamentary secretary to the justice minister said that an extension beyond the twelve-month period would be requested because that was not enough time to deal with the issue. Then, he "backtracked."
3. The Liberals proposed an all-party committee to deal with the question, but this was defeated by the Conservatives, who offered no alternative other then "a vague promise to hold public consultations."

Consultation with the public, said Picard, was merely "foot-dragging." He concluded:

> To refresh the memories of our too-busy-to-draft-laws legislators: In the Carter case, the top court struck down two sections of the Criminal Code: Section 14, which says that "no person is entitled to consent to have death inflicted upon him" and section 241(b), which says that anyone who "aids or abets a person to commit suicide" commits a crime.
>
> In short, the Supreme Court said that it is unconstitutional to deny gravely ill patients choice in how they die. But it also placed some fairly strict parameters on who can choose to hasten death — only a competent adult with an irremediable condition that causes enduring, intolerable suffering.
>
> The court said competency can be judged easily enough — after all, physicians make those

decisions every day. The ruling is clear that assisted death must be voluntary, and it cannot be chosen by children or those who are incompetent. The only unresolved issues are whether the law should apply to mature minors who have the right to make other treatment decisions and whether someone can invoke assisted death at a later time with an advanced directive (*Globe and Mail*, March 3, 2015).

ANOTHER SLIPPERY SLOPE?

In effect, the task as to how the twelve-month "grace period" will be used largely seems to be in the hands of the federal government. Yet, as Picard suggests, this is strange. After all, while criminal law is a federal matter under the Constitution, health care is within the authority of the provinces.

In enacting Bill 52, Quebec set out criteria that would allow physician-assisted death similar to the parameters stated the Supreme Court of Canada in *Carter*. Further, the Quebec law provides for end-of-life palliative care. And, toward that end, Quebec provides for a commission to monitor the law. A register is established for patients to file their advance directives relating to end-of-life care.

Through such patient directives, the individual sets a path for her/his medical team well in advance of any later stage of individual incompetence.

In North America, Oregon has had physician-assisted end-of-life laws since 1997 (called Death with Dignity). Courtney Campbell, a medical ethics expert who teaches at Oregon State University, said that most of his students (undergraduates) "wonder what's wrong with the other States in the United States ...

that don't have something like [Oregon's end-of-life law]? It's just become part of the landscape here."

The Oregon law requires that the person seeking assisted death be fatally ill with an estimation of less than six months of life remaining before she/he is likely to die. A doctor signs a prescription for a lethal drug that the individual must individually take.

The Oregon law requires detailed reporting. The death rates have climbed slowly since the law was enacted — from sixteen in 1971 to seventy-one in 2013 (two in every one thousand deaths in the state). Sixty-three doctors gave 122 lethal prescriptions in 2013. About a quarter of those receiving such prescriptions never used them (*National Post*, February 6, 2015).

PALLIATIVE CARE: A LIMITED SUPPLY

For more than 70 percent of Canadians, palliative care is not available. Following the Carter decision, Harvey Max Chochinov, director of the Manitoba Palliative Care Research Unit, wrote:

> There, the choices will come down to settling for sub-optimal care; dislocating from friends and family to seek out better care elsewhere; or, if one is so inclined, considering medically hastened death.
>
> We are about to become a country that extends patients the right to a hastened death, but offers no legislative guarantees or assurances that they will be well looked after until they die.
>
> As Canada deliberates its response to the court's decision, federal and provincial governments will need to make substantive investments in hospice and palliative care in order to offer patients and families choices that are equitable,

compassionate and real (*Toronto Star*, February 18, 2015).

The Canadian Medical Association (CMA) has called for the creation of a national palliative care plan in the report "End-of-Life Care: A National Dialogue." Dr. Louis Hugo Francescutti, CMA president, stated that any legislation allowing physician-assisted suicide does not negate the need for proper palliative care services. He said: "Canadians expect more of the health care system. They expect more of our politicians to provide access to quality palliative care for all Canadians, regardless of what your postal code is" (*Globe and Mail*, June 10, 2014).

REFERENCES AND FURTHER READING

Arvay Q.C, Joseph J., and Alison Latimer. "Cost Strategies for Litigants: The Significance of *R. v. Caron.*" *Supreme Court Law Review* (2nd edition) 2011: 54.

Blackwell, Tom. "Avoid a 'Wild West' of Mercy Killing, Say Those Who've Grown Up With Assisted-Suicide Law." *National Post*, February 6, 2015.

Chochinov, Harvey Max. "Canada Failing on Palliative Care." *Toronto Star*, February 18, 2015.

Dale, Michelle. "Palliative Care, Done Right: Relief for Pain, Solace for the Spirit." *Globe and Mail*, February 6, 2015.

Giles, David. "Understanding the Charter's Notwithstanding Clause." globalnews.ca, February 6, 2015.

Goldman, Dr. Brian. "Palliative Care vs Assisted Suicide: A False Dichotomy?" CBC.ca/radio, December 4, 2014.

Picard, André. "How are MPs Too Busy to Correct Right-to-Die Injustice?" *Globe and Mail*, March 3, 2015.

Weeks, Carly. "Canada Needs National Palliative Care Plan, CMA Urges." *Globe and Mail*, June 10, 2014.

INDEX

Also in the Understanding Canadian Law Series

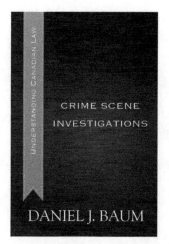

Crime Scene Investigations
Daniel J. Baum

When police are called in to investigate a crime, what powers and limitations apply to them? What are their rights to question strangers, search without warrants, or detain individuals who might become suspects? *Crime Scene Investigations* breaks down the Supreme Court's decisions on questions like these into clear and practical terms.

Police need to be vigilant, since the line between a lawful search and an improper one can be dangerously thin, and officers can be held accountable for any wrongdoing, intentional or not. The controversy surrounding such techniques as "stop-and-frisk" sweeps and compulsory DNA testing underscores the importance of understanding the legal dimensions of police powers. Because interactions between law enforcement officers and civilians are often charged with complexities, *Crime Scene Investigations* provides a level-headed guide, indispensable for those on either side of an investigation.

Available at your favourite bookseller

Visit us at

Dundurn.com
@dundurnpress
Facebook.com/dundurnpress
Pinterest.com/dundurnpress